W0018459

SAGE was founded in 1965 by Sara Miller McCune to support the dissemination of usable knowledge by publishing innovative and high-quality research and teaching content. Today, we publish over 900 journals, including those of more than 400 learned societies, more than 800 new books per year, and a growing range of library products including archives, data, case studies, reports, and video. SAGE remains majority-owned by our founder, and after Sara's lifetime will become owned by a charitable trust that secures our continued independence.

Los Angeles | London | New Delhi | Singapore | Washington DC | Melbourne

ADVANCE PRAISE

Pathak-Shelat and Bhatia's new book *Raising a Humanist: Conscious Parenting in an Increasingly Fragmented World* provides a much-needed exploration of how adults can guide children to become empathetic, tolerant and critically reflective humans in an ever-changing technological landscape. As scholars and parents, we applaud the authors for delving deep into some of the most challenging questions of our times in a rigorous and thoughtful yet accessible manner. Concepts are carefully unpacked, illustrated with 'real-world' scenarios and framed in ways that adults and kids can talk about together. Especially well done are the calls of the authors to move outside our echo chambers and genuinely engage in dialogue and active listening. This book is essential reading for anyone interested in parenting in these politically complex and technologically disruptive times.

Christine L. Garlough, *Professor, Department of Gender & Women's Studies, Head of the Folklore Program, University of Wisconsin-Madison and* **Dhavan V. Shah,** *Louis A. & Mary E. Maier-Bascom Professor, School of Journalism and Mass Communication, University of Wisconsin-Madison*

Raising a Humanist is a must-read, especially for parents, educators and concerned citizens who are hungry for a radical vision of the world that we will leave for our children, not driven innately by fear and suspicion, but from the point of well-being, empathy, pleasure, curiosity and engagement with rich and diverse people, platforms and places. This book is a refreshing departure from the tiresome 'how to' books imposed on caregivers, as you see guilt and fear taking a rightful back seat to more nuanced, critical and creative conversations that generate excitement for how we would like to see the world turn for the better.

Payal Arora, *Professor and Chair in Technology, Values, and Global Media Cultures, Erasmus University Rotterdam, and Author of* The Next Billion Users: Digital Life Beyond the West

As a scholar who reflects on contemporary media discourse, as an academic leader who is responsible for shaping young minds and as a parent who is raising a child, this text had me at its title. The book addresses key questions and concepts informing the experiences of parents. It mainstreams the power of initiating difficult conversations and discussions, guided by a strong yet sensitive rationale at its core. A must-read for everyone, academic or non-academic, for we all raise ideas, beliefs and people. The book will not only make its readers more self-aware of their personal and social ecosystems but will also extend itself to being a reference, sometimes even a toolkit, to negotiate with questions and everyday practices in their journeys of raising tolerant youngsters.

Ruchi Kher Jaggi, *PhD, Professor and Director, Symbiosis Institute of Media and Communication India*

Pathak-Shelat and Bhatia's book *Raising a Humanist* comes handy in this VUCA world to parents when the pandemic has added to the parenting pangs. The lucid case studies and the real-life examples in the book make an interesting read. The book not only sketches the social divide but also remediates it by addressing its concerns. The book talks of the nuances of religion and prejudice in the most succinct manner. One cannot miss the imagery drawn through the use of the concept of 'echo chambers'. The book also suggests a few simple practices to refurbish the social fabric, which, if adopted, would ease the process of raising conscientious and empathetic children. Debunking some of the parenting myths with reality-check exercises is a frosting on the cake. The spaces provided for pausing compels one to introspect, which is very crucial for a parent.

The question is, 'Should you rock the boat or not?' Do read this book to find that out. I assure the ride is worth taking.

Dr Heena Rachh, *Educationist and Thought Leader, Principal at Global Indian International School, Abu Dhabi*

The book *Raising a Humanist: Conscious Parenting in an Increasingly Fragmented World* aims to help parents debunk stereotypes, biases, mental conditioning about gender, caste, religion and class. Children from a young age are conditioned into stereotypical and biased ways of thinking if parents are not alert. The book not only raises the right questions but also offers solutions by providing a deeper understanding of popular culture and the role of the media in gender, religious, caste and class portrayals! Most importantly, the authors tell us how to unlearn and re-learn as parents first so that we can raise children who can walk through life with confidence and compassion. This book should be in every parent's must-read list! I strongly recommend this book not only to parents but to anyone who wants to shape young minds in meaningful ways.

Falguni Vasavada, *Professor and Chair, Strategic Marketing Area, MICA, Ahmedabad*

Professor Manisha Pathak-Shelat and Kiran Bhatia bring to the subject of 'parenting' a lens which is both deep and accessible. It is a book that speaks to one of the most pressing issues of our time—how to raise a child in this polarized and conflicted world—and does so with insight and wisdom. As academics, the authors use a lens that is scholarly in its multidisciplinary sweep while never straying too far from rooting the book in everyday experiences.

Santosh Desai, *Columnist, Media Critic and Bestselling Author; Managing Director and CEO, Futurebrands India*

RAISING a
HUMANIST

Thank you for choosing a SAGE product!
If you have any comment, observation or feedback,
I would like to personally hear from you.

Please write to me at **contactceo@sagepub.in**

Vivek Mehra, Managing Director and CEO, SAGE India.

Bulk Sales

SAGE India offers special discounts
for purchase of books in bulk.
We also make available special imprints
and excerpts from our books on demand.

For orders and enquiries, write to us at

Marketing Department
SAGE Publications India Pvt Ltd
B1/I-1, Mohan Cooperative Industrial Area
Mathura Road, Post Bag 7
New Delhi 110044, India

E-mail us at **marketing@sagepub.in**

Subscribe to our mailing list
Write to **marketing@sagepub.in**

This book is also available as an e-book.

MANISHA PATHAK-SHELAT
KIRAN VINOD BHATIA

RAISING *a* HUMANIST

Conscious Parenting in an Increasingly Fragmented World

Los Angeles | London | New Delhi
Singapore | Washington DC | Melbourne

First published in 2021 by

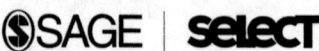

SAGE Publications India Pvt Ltd
B1/I-1 Mohan Cooperative Industrial Area
Mathura Road, New Delhi 110 044, India
www.sagepub.in

SAGE Publications Inc
2455 Teller Road
Thousand Oaks, California 91320, USA

SAGE Publications Ltd
1 Oliver's Yard, 55 City Road
London EC1Y 1SP, United Kingdom

SAGE Publications Asia-Pacific Pte Ltd
18 Cross Street #10-10/11/12
China Square Central
Singapore 048423

Published by Vivek Mehra for SAGE Publications India Pvt. Ltd. Typeset in 11/14.5 pt Minion Pro by Fidus Design Pvt. Ltd, Chandigarh.

Library of Congress Control Number: 2021932745

ISBN: 978-93-5388-775-9 (PB)

SAGE Team: Manisha Mathews, Satvinder Kaur, Madhurima Thapa
Illustration Credit: Mehul Prajapati

CONTENTS

FOREWORD

If ever there was a book for its time, this is it. Our planet is in turmoil. Our Earth is in turmoil. Humanity is in turmoil. Global instability at this scale shows us that the old order and the old way of doing things are not working. We need a new way forward, and this will change when the next generation thinks, acts, believes and feels differently than the one before it. For this to happen, a new conscious parenting style needs to be adopted and *Raising a Humanist: Conscious Parenting in an Increasingly Fragmented World* is a book that parents can use as a guide and handbook.

Most parents know and feel that they want a different future for their children than the one that currently exists. There is a lot of information on the web from how to change a tyre to how to build a bomb. For parents, there is a lot of information on how to teach their children to read, write and do math. Very little is available on how to make the children more tolerant, fairer, more peaceful, more loving and more humane.

The authors, two communication scholars representing two generations, take you on a parenting journey, an invitation to raise your children in a way that makes the world more peaceful and joyful for all of humanity. If you want to leave a legacy, I urge you not to leave it by gifting the world a child who is more competitive, more ferocious and more financially successful. Gift the world a child who has the passion for finding ways and solutions to change this chaotic, violent, and intolerant world.

This book invites you to reinvent parenting where you use critical thinking, media, art and technology to move from a state of helplessness and fear to that of action and empowerment. Within the scope of this remarkable book, the authors bring insights from global research, experience and literature, presented in a jargon-free language, and provide practical tips and pointers to rethink our daily experiences. *Raising a Humanist* puts you in a driver's seat and guides you all along the path to raising happy, confident and humane children in whose hands our beautiful world will remain safe.

I urge all parents to step off the treadmill of living life as we know it and to pause and read this book with the mindful presence it deserves. Make a conscious decision as a parent to bring awareness, mindfulness and consciousness into your parenting. Let this be your legacy.

Lina Ashar
Educationist, Entrepreneur, Writer
Founder, Kangaroo Kids Preschool, Mumbai, and
Billabong High International School, Noida

PREFACE

This book is a conversation—with us and with the parents who are riding the parenting roller coaster every day. It is our response to what we find disturbing in our society and our attempt to co-create something better with you.

While both of us are active academics and researchers, we do not practise our profession in an ivory tower. We cherish our connection with parents, teachers and young people in a variety of personal and professional roles. We completely understand that our realities are not black and white—that is why we do not call this a 'how to' guide or a 'parenting advice book' where we preach ideals from a pedestal. This book is the beginning of a long conversation on parenting and nurturing young people in times of uncertainties. Being a humanist could be difficult in today's times: confusing, full of contradictions and sometimes conflicts. Raising a humanist is still more difficult because it involves shaping and influencing the lives of those who are very precious to us. As a scholar, Manisha is a strong ally of women's movement and right to voice, but as a mother she often worries when her daughter openly expresses her views on critical issues and questions dominant thinking. Similarly, though Kiran was raised in a nurturing family where equality was taught and practised, she had to unlearn a lot of patriarchal bias that she had inherited from her society and community, and the unlearning process continues. We have drawn from our lived realities—work, family and experiences—to design this book. We acknowledge that it may create some sense of discomfort in our readers. It may raise more questions than it can answer. If that happens, we will believe that our work has been a success. We have discussed a range of topics, from echo chambers operating along the vectors of gender, class, caste and religion to exploring more contemporary possibilities of using art and technology for practicing tolerance.

We do not have easy answers to many burning questions, for example, questions about territory and rights. Should we stop others from entering our habitats and discriminate against them just because we arrived before them to that area? At the same time, should we take over our host community and change their generation-old ways of living just because we are larger in number and the sheer number makes us more powerful than them? Similarly, as people who give equal respect and stake to different communities, how should we respond to those who justify the abuse and ill-treatment of certain individuals in the name of culture and tradition? When do we take a stand? When and how should we encourage our children to take a stand? We suggest several tried and tested options in the book but leave the final decision to you. You are the best judge of your situation. And we completely understand that the safety and well-being of your children are the most important considerations.

We can, however, say a few things with confidence. The world can be made a better place for our children when all differences are not seen as a threat, when violence is diffused through dialogue and critical thinking is encouraged rather than punished. Nudged by the global literature on discrimination and social justice, we have constantly examined and re-examined our experiences of discrimination as well as our privileges as upper class, upper caste, well-educated, Indian urban women. We encourage you to do so. We believe that raising the 'why' question while examining every accepted practice of discrimination and 'why not' while attempting to embrace every progressive alternative is a powerful first step.

Critical thinking, empathy and the readiness to engage with different viewpoints have to be a gradual and a lifelong process—beginning with ourselves, including our children and extending it to our larger social circles. Of course, there is a place and a time for everything. This book is not about provoking you to ruin every dinner party, family gathering and movie night by jumping into strident arguments. We have also observed that not everyone has the same articulation capacity or willingness to debate these issues at all times and in all places. We must learn to adjust our tactics and our pace and become pros in the art of persuasion. Developing sound emotional and relational intelligence in our children would make them more successful in eventually bringing about change in our societies.

We thank you for choosing to walk with us through the chapters. Here is to our children and our beautiful planet, the only home we have!

ACKNOWLEDGEMENTS

This book is a labour of love; it is our sincere effort to translate years of training as academicians into ideas, suggestions and provocations designed to invite more people to 'reimagine parenting' in a world witnessing unprecedented changes, chaos and fears.

Our deepest gratitude will always be reserved for our students who have nourished our understanding of society and the world. Although they appear as pseudo names in the book for privacy concerns, they are the foundation guiding this book project. Our students have helped us identify gaps in our thinking and model our approach in ways that more people can access academic research. We strongly believe in democratizing education so that more people can draw from our work and writing.

All the events we describe as anecdotes are faithful representations of our experiences in classrooms and in the field. Undertaking such a massive task of un/learning through writing was made possible by the unending support we received at our academic institutions. We are extremely grateful for the rigorously intellectual environment and our colleagues at MICA, Ahmedabad, and the School of Journalism and Mass Communication, University of Wisconsin–Madison, USA. Conversations that we have had at both these institutions have shaped much of the book's content.

We are very fortunate in the enthusiasm of Manisha Mathews, our editor at SAGE Publications, who believed in our project and encouraged us to write a lucid, hard-hitting and critical text. Her comments, insights and rigorous editorial reports were instrumental in tightening the final manuscript. She responded with meticulous sharpness and rigour to the various drafts of writing, which culminated in our book *Raising a Humanist: Conscious Parenting in an Increasingly Fragmented World*.

Although this book is a collaborative endeavour between Manisha Pathak-Shelat and Kiran Vinod Bhatia, there is a delicate poignancy in the fact that both drew immense support and love from their personal circles of family, friends and colleagues at different stages of this project.

MANISHA PATHAK-SHELAT

Gratitude and love to my parents—Late Professor Chandravdan Pathak and Professor Yogini Pathak—for an enriching childhood and youth where no topic was a taboo during dinner table conversations, for the love of books and travel and for being my unconditional support system, and to my spouse, Uday, for surrounding me with care, love, companionship, conversations and tea and for being proud of my work. He keeps me going. Thanks to my daughter, Revati, for constantly reminding me that she values and admires my work (and my humour!) and does not need me to be a helicopter parent. This independent and lively young woman keeps me on my mental toes, challenging my every half-baked argument and giving me fresh perspectives, fun and hope for our future generation. She also keeps my laptop glitch-free. Thanks to my home help, Tara *bahen* and Usha *bahen*, for freeing the time I need to work on my various writing projects by helping our home and kitchen run smoothly. I would also like to express my gratitude to my extended family and friends who remind me that you can love and have fun together even with diverse opinions and choices.

KIRAN VINOD BHATIA

I am grateful for the extensive network of friends and colleagues who have accompanied me to coffee houses and salad bars, and for walks on the Lakeshore. I have had remarkable conversations with Ben Kreimer, Devpriya Chakravarty, Kruthika Kamath, Matt Minich and Shreenita Ghosh. These conversations have given me the courage to speak, write and teach what I truly believe in. Shafiq Ahmed, on the other hand, has been the one dragging me away from books and research and into endless fits of laughter and frivolity.

I owe a profound debt to Julian Clark for his unwavering support, encouragement and companionship. From scattered pages, hours of procrastination and unfinished ideas to boat rides, TV shows and food deliveries—he has been the cornerstone of my sanity.

Payal, my big-little sister, has walked me through the most difficult phases of my life. *Didi* has provided me with a safe corner in this ever-changing world. She has also given me another family in Shona and Ravi. No matter where I go, I will always have a home with my sister.

I owe an intellectual debt to my parents, Neelam Bhatia and Vinod Bhatia, for actively engaging and supporting my politics, aspirations and experiences. They encourage me to identify the discontinuities in my knowledge and reasoning, to practise my beliefs and to always question the authority, both at home and outside. Most importantly, they taught me to accept my vulnerabilities as a sign of empathy rather than weakness. My parents helped me find and build my own place in the world, and they supported my dreams and ambitions. To them and them alone, I dedicate this book and all my happiness, success and joy.

CHAPTER 1

What Is Your Child's World View?

These are challenging times. On the one side, new technologies, material and scientific development, global exposure and our rising standard of living make parenting an exciting adventure. At the same time, if you are a parent and/or teacher, dreaming of raising your children and students in a peaceful and fair world, witnessing chaos, violence and intolerance might cause confusion, fear and helplessness.

As a society, we have made huge strides in advancing human rights in many ways, but we still have a long way to go. In India and globally, we are witnessing a rising culture of violence and a growing disrespect for differences with regard to religious–caste–gender–race identities and lifestyle choices: Individuals are lynched to death for their caste and religious identities, wealthy parents refuse poor students' entry into same school where their children are studying, those with dark skin are humiliated due to an undying obsession for fair skin, young students are using the Internet, especially social media, to harass and bully others under the cloak of invisibility, individuals with alternative gender identities are constantly abused and humiliated, and young people, especially girls, are increasingly falling prey to upholding the ideal but unreal beauty standards promoted by the entertainment industry. Those who feel upset by these happenings and want to speak out feel vulnerable and unsafe for the fear of verbal and at times physical attacks. They make an uneasy peace with the situation.

This book strives to address these fears and confusion and walks parents and teachers through the path of raising tolerant and peace-loving children who respect those who are 'different' from them, to speak up against violence, hatred and injustice, while at the same time being alert to their own vulnerability and to their own well-being. We hope that this book will help you in introducing young minds to the possibilities of peaceful coexistence in societies with people of diverse social, cultural, religious and economic backgrounds.

To embark on this path, we must first understand how children learn who they are, what their identities are and about their roles/positions in the society through their families, the media they consume and their schools. In order to understand how parents and family influence the way children make sense of the world, let us take the following quiz. The results will shed light on how we, as adults, nurture our children every day.

QUIZ TIME

A. Do your children have friends who are from a different religious community?

1. No. I don't think it is advisable to allow young children to befriend people who have a different religion. They might get influenced.

2. No. Children are gullible, and if they are exposed to different beliefs, they might want to leave our religion.

3. Yes. I have always encouraged my children to meet new people and experience different lifestyles.

B. Who is considered to be a breadwinner of your family?

1. Men in the family.

2. Mother/both the parents.

3. Each member effectively contributes in some way to ensure that the kitchen is stocked, the house is warm and there are books on the shelf.

C. Who should manage the finances for the family?

1. The husband.

2. Father in-law.

3. Both partners have equal stake in the process of financial management.

D. Do you expect your son/s to learn how to take care of their rooms and homes?

1. No. I am supposed to provide them with all the care and comfort so that they can focus on studies.

2. Only sometimes because they don't need to do these menial tasks. We have servants. They must focus on their career and personal development.

3. Always. Every individual should be able to take care of their homes and basic needs.

E. Which family members are responsible for kitchen chores and other household works?

1. The mother and daughter/s.

2. Mother and father/sons.

3. The entire family takes turns to manage the house.

F. Do you share your utensils with your house helps?

1. No. House helps are not clean given the nature of their jobs and so we cannot allow them to eat and drink from the same utensils.

2. We have separate utensils for everyone in the house including the house helps.

3. Yes. Why should we have separately marked utensils for them?

G. Do you often use religious (*mullah, topi, kafir*), caste (*bhangi, barwaad, chuda*) and/or gender (*motherfucker/sisterfucker/chutiya*) slurs in your families?

   1. Sometimes. I try not to use it in front of the children, but sometimes my tongue slips.

   2. I don't use it in front of my children, but these words are part of my vocabulary.

   3. Never. I am not at all comfortable using these words.

H. How often do you accept your mistakes in front of your children and apologize for them?

   1. I don't think I should apologize as a parent.

   2. I don't apologize or accept my mistakes but try to make up for them in a different way.

   3. I always apologize and ask for forgiveness.

I. What do you think about the new regulation that a few seats in all private schools should be reserved for children from a low economic class? Would you be happy for your child to have these children as friends?

   1. I won't be very excited. Children who belong to different backgrounds won't be able to mingle well.

   2. I am comfortable if the school accepts children from a lower economic background. I will, however, not allow my children to befriend them after school hours.

   3. Yes. I would like for my children to be exposed to different realities and family backgrounds.

Once you have marked your answers, calculate your total score using the serial number of the options selected as the value of your response. The scorecard is given as follows.

SCORECARD

Below 15	Need to immediately work on your outlook
15–27	Need to rethink on several issues
27 and above	Keep up the progressive thinking

Becoming a critical and conscious adult is a life-long process. The term 'parent' or 'teacher' is a verb and not a noun. It isn't merely who we are. It is a process that we continuously engage in and work on. We are always in the 'process of being a parent', which means that we must consciously evaluate and improve our methods of nurturing children. Regardless of the score, this book will help you critically examine your engagement with children and draw from a wide array of resources to improve your style and pedagogy.

MIRRORING THE ADULTS

Parenting is exciting, but it is never an easy task. We want our children to thrive and grow up in a caring and nurturing society. As parents, we feel vulnerable and anxious as news of violence, hate crimes, abuse and discrimination surround us. We also helplessly come to terms with situations where our own children are either the objects of hatred, bullying or discrimination or those who unwittingly perpetuate the cycle of hatred. Can we change this? Yes, at least to some extent, and that is what this book is all about; but for that, the first step is to understand how our communities and larger societies become toxic instead of supportive.

Let us be honest. Accepting something that is 'different' is not always easy. We often look with suspicion at people who seem different, who a different lifestyle or culture or who have a different way of seeing the world. Realizing that we—parents, teachers, family members, and other adults—are responsible for sowing seeds of bias and prejudice in the minds of young people can be unsettling, especially when we love them and care for them. As a result, most of us refuse to evaluate our stake in the process of raising children who are biased, intolerant and scared of interacting with others who are different from themselves. Also, many of us are unaware of our own personal bias towards other individuals, belief systems, practices and processes.

Does the following conversation ring a familiar bell?

> Palak (entering the house after a day at school as her mother is entertaining some guests): That Chirag is a donkey. He didn't select me in his handball team during the sports class and I had to sit outside. I couldn't play. Let me become the captain once; I'll make sure that the *bhangi* knows his place.
>
> Nita (is angry listening to her daughter abuse and use caste slurs in front of guests): Watch your tongue. Is this how you are supposed to speak in front of people?
>
> Palak (looking confused): What did I say? You call him a *bhangi* all the time. And donkey is a normal word. It isn't even an abuse anymore. You call us donkey all day!
>
> Nita (evidently embarrassed): Shut up and go freshen up. I'll serve lunch.
>
> Palak (withdrawing into the room): It is okay for you to say such things, and when I say the same things you behave like a snake has bitten you!

This is an excerpt from a conversation between a 10-year-old girl and her mother, and such conversations are not unfamiliar to us. As is evident, the girl is a keen observer and a quick learner. She listens closely to her mother and internalizes everything that the mother says about other people in their neighbourhoods and communities. The mother is her window to the world.

Children are keen observers. They consciously and subconsciously model the behaviour of adults around them—their actions, words, thought processes and emotions. During the formative years of a child's development, adults, especially parents and family members, act as a bridge linking children with the world outside. Adults initiate children in everyday activities, belief systems, values, codes of conduct and ethics, and thus help them understand how they should behave in relation to people, places and communities.

This is part of the process of socialization, that is, the process through which children are trained to enact their role in the world. Children learn who they are as they take up social roles in their lives. For instance, children brought up in religious families begin to engage with the concept of 'God' from an early age and are trained to perform actions that articulate their relationship with God. They participate in religious rituals, perform certain rites, develop a particular lifestyle that influence their food preferences, clothing choices and other everyday activities. These everyday practices help them cultivate opinions about the world. Religion becomes one of the lenses through which they look at themselves and others. It is a similar process with caste, gender and other identities.

The process of socialization, thus, is multi-layered and very complex. It broadly operates at three levels:

1. *Individual:* At this level, children learn about their social roles and the accepted modes of performing these within families and societies. For instance, children may adopt several social roles such as those of a religious subject, a student, a family member, a citizen and a friend. As they learn how to behave from within the boundaries of these roles, they look for examples in adults around them and perceive their adults as role models. They study their parents' behaviour, for instance, to identify socially acceptable ways to perform each of these roles within their communities. Observing adults in their surroundings helps them understand how they should

define themselves: Who are they—are they Hindus/Muslims/Christians? Others? Are they upper-caste/lower-caste Hindus? Are they seen as rich or poor? What is their gender and how should they act like a girl/boy/other? What are their familial, social, educational responsibilities and expectations? It is through socialization that children develop a notion of the 'self'.

2. *Others:* The notion of self is defined in relation to others in the society. For instance, if a girl child performs her role as a daughter, she regulates her behaviour in relation to the parents or grandparents in the family. Right from a young age, children are taught what they can do, watch, feel and say in accordance with the norms and rules normalized within societies.

   Girls often face more family restrictions in the Indian society. For instance, in many families, women are not encouraged to participate in major financial decisions and investments but are required to learn home chores. Girls in such families are never encouraged to learn financial skills, while boys start taking interest in these matters at an early age. A boy also internalizes his role as a future primary breadwinner for the family and assumes that the kitchen is not his domain. As is evident, the brother and the sister have learnt how to situate themselves in relation to the other 'gender'. The problem begins when this creates hierarchies in the society where one role is labelled superior to the other. For example, home chores and financial skills are both important life skills, but household work and labour are considered inferior to financial competencies.

3. *Community:* Each community creates a set of rules, regulations and norms to ensure that individuals behave in ways that reinforce the authority of their community. These communities are a local network of family, friends, professionals, neighbours and acquaintances who belong to the

same social groups, based on class, caste, religion, gender and so on. Some examples of such networks can include specific Church denominations, caste associations, *mahila mandals* or clubs. Children interact with many such communities from a young age and learn how to abide by the rules and norms that these communities sanction. Also, parents often refer to these community expectations while socializing their children within set societal norms.

On the basis of their observations of how adults in their lives behave, children learn to internalize biases towards others, practise hatred against individuals who have a different lifestyle and design violent ways of punishing, abusing and reprimanding those who challenge their world views, faiths and beliefs.

THE UNKNOWN IS SCARY

We often protect our children from diverse interactions because we have learnt to associate strangers with danger! In order to keep our children safe, we encourage them to avoid any interaction with people who are not like us, who may 'corrupt' our innocent children, especially those we consider inferior to us. Of course, the risks are real and, in the chapters that follow, we also talk about how to recognize and deal with risks while broadening the social circles of our families.

'Different' doesn't always mean bad or evil, superior or inferior. Such an attitude is damaging our social fabric and making many people miserable. For the sake of peace and development in our society, we need to raise children who can happily navigate and enjoy a diverse and multicultural society while acknowledging and respecting their own roots and cultures. For this, it is important to understand how children develop a world view, that is, how they cultivate opinions about other individuals and how they learn to engage with different people in their societies. There are three major institutions—family, school and media—in a society which socialize children. Examining how these institutions influence and shape our children's world view will help us identify new ways of raising our children so that they grow into individuals who are prepared to ask important questions, enact compassion and work towards establishing social justice in their societies.

THE BIG THREE: HOW FAMILY, SCHOOL AND MEDIA SHAPE OUR CHILDREN

Family, school and media are the three most important building blocks constituting children's world view. While families and schools allow children to learn and practise norms and codes of conduct acceptable to the communities and countries in which they live, the media is a channel that connects children's local environments and the outside world. Children's perceptions of how power and politics work in the world, how to make sense of realities which they cannot experience first-hand, their mental images of people and places and their perception of their own place in the world are largely influenced by the media.

Let us look at an example. Young girls learn about gender roles dominant in their immediate communities from family members, teachers, friends and peers through routine interactions. Many families and communities in India, for instance, want their girls to be fair because only fair skin is considered to be beautiful. Fair becomes synonymous with lovely. In many schools, fair girls often act as female protagonists in theatre activities and other school programmes, such as cultural dance performances and video making. Many young girls are raised on a staple diet of the following aspirations.

Fair is lovely!

- You must try to make your skin look fair.
- If you have a dark skin, you must resort to chemical treatments/facials/and other cosmetic procedures to lighten your skin colour.
- Girls should not play sports because exposure to the sun will darken their skin and make them look ugly.
- Girls who have a dark skin shouldn't wear certain colours because those colours will make their skin look darker.
- For matrimony, only fair girls are in demand. If your daughter has dark skin, it will be difficult to find a match for her.

As is evident, families and communities instil in children the obsession for fair skin through daily communication and practices. Gradually, it also translates into discrimination against dark-skinned people, that is, considering them less valuable or beautiful. This obsession over fair skin is then reinforced through media narratives where famous celebrities endorse beauty products designed to make girls look fair and lovely. The media acts as a bridge between children's local experiences and the trends and practices dominant in the outside world. It is, however, important to realize that popular culture in the outside world of children and everyday experiences in their immediate surroundings happen simultaneously and constantly feed off each other.

As shown in Figure 1.1, children are socialized on the basis of an interaction between what they observe and practise at home, in schools and communities and how these patterns of thoughts and actions are normalized and justified through media and popular culture. What is significant in this spiral of socialization

Figure 1.1: Children's World View as an Interaction between the In/Out-worlds

is the interdependence of these two worlds. Let us look at how the three building blocks constitute the world view of children.

Home: Observing, Learning, Practising

Homes are rich learning sites where children are introduced to four crucial social identities: religion, gender, caste and class. Let us look at the following interaction between a 12-year-old boy, his sister and his grandmother in a Muslim household.

Boy (demanding that his sister hand over the TV remote to him): Enough with watching your serials. Give me the remote (almost snatching it from her hands as she tries to stop him). I have to finish the last stage of my game.

Sister (visibly irritated): I am not giving you the remote. I was here at the TV set first. You wait for your turn.

Boy (roughing up with his sister trying to snatch the remote): I am going to tell father that you weren't wearing your hijab after school today. Give me the remote, or you'll get a thrashing from father.

Grandmother (shouting at the sister): What are you doing in the drawing room? Who will help your mother? It is dinner time. Come to the kitchen.

As is evident, the grandmother encouraged both the children to practise their religious and gender identities while trying to resolve their conflict over a TV remote. In this case, children have learned what it means to be a boy/girl in their family and what is expected of a good Muslim girl. The authority of the boy over the TV remote is symptomatic of a larger issue in a society where men have greater and unrestricted access to information, opinion, money and other resources. You can see that these patriarchal practices prevailing in the society manifest in the form of day-to-day interactions among family members. The girl is coaxed into accepting the authority of the patriarchal figure in her family through small acts of submission, in this instance the handing over of the TV remote to her brother. On the other hand, the boy knows only too well how important it is for children to perform their religious identities in public spaces such as schools and community areas. His gendered role as a male member of the society intersects with his religious identity, and he is convinced that his sister's action of frequenting public spaces without a hijab is considered 'wrong/abnormal' according to his religious community. In compelling the sister to hand over the TV remote, he has learnt an acceptable way of performing both patriarchy and religion within the walls of his house. This learning will translate and overflow into other places, sites, experiences and people. For example, in the future, when he encounters a girl with an independent mind, his response could be to put her down or, in extreme cases, behave violently towards her.

School: A Social Playground

Schools are social playgrounds where children learn social behaviour, relations, attitudes and values. There are three reasons why schools are so instrumental in the development of children as responsible adults and members of the society.

1. In school, children learn through peer interaction, which is a very powerful means of training children as members of a social community. Many studies argue that children are more receptive to certain attitudes, values and behaviours when they observe their peers performing those in social settings. Schools provide a fertile site for these peer interactions to unfold.

2. In the formative years, teachers are one of the strongest influencers, and children model their behaviour either to imitate the teachers or to please them. In either case, teachers encourage their students to perform certain social behaviours that they consider important. Sometimes, these social behaviours may reinforce gender, religious, caste and class bias in classrooms and normalize the prevailing stereotypes.

3. Children spend most of their time at school, especially in India, where school timings extend to approximately 7 to 8 hours per day. As a result, experiences that children have in their school influence them in significant ways. Schools

also function as 'proxy sites' for children to experience the outside world. Children bring to the classroom their family socialization, social identities, beliefs and values. These diverse realities and identities interact with each other in classrooms, and children's engagement in these interactions informs their attitudes and beliefs towards those who have different lifestyle practices. It is, therefore, crucial to identify classrooms as a place where children experience the differences prevailing in their societies for the first time. Classrooms are also the place where children can learn the critical skills required to live with these differences and even enjoy such interactions.

Children's socialization is braided with their school experiences. Schools are a proxy playground for several social differences to coexist; they can be defined as a mini-social setting designed to help children understand the social realities existing in the outside world from a safe distance.

Media: Constructing Social Realities

The media often acts as a lens through which children witness and participate in the outside world. It performs two critical functions in socializing children. First, it informs and influences the aspirations of children in relation to how they should position themselves in their societies. Second, it legitimizes several social practices and interactions. For instance, young children who have been raised on the staple diet of item numbers often sing, dance and appreciate these songs in their routines. We observe that many child contestants on children's talent shows in India such as 'Dance India Dance', 'India's Got Talent' and others are encouraged to perform seductively on item number songs to become more popular and get more votes. Repeated and continuous exposure to such TV content normalizes the act of sexualizing children's bodies and encourages children to look at themselves using the same lens. They may also develop the fear that if they do not do this, the attention and love they are receiving will be withdrawn.

It is important to note that the role of the media is not limited to just representing the society as it is. It not only selects trending issues of popular interest but also encourages individuals to understand these issues in specific ways. For instance, for years, item number songs in Bollywood movies were not criticized for sexualizing and objectifying female bodies in harmful ways. Also, the portrayals of protagonists or female leads in Bollywood movies as fair and thin reinforce the stereotype that a girl must be fair and thin to be successful in life. In many movies, their role and character are ornamental; that is, they provide diversion and comic-relief through extremely sexualized songs and dances. Media portrayals thus compel us to think of beauty among women in a limited sense—fair, thin, unquestioning and yielding, and to believe that their role in the society is limited to 'serving the men'.

Media often represents a selected part of reality and what they want to show. For instance, during a religious conflict, voices that are strident, violent and radical always draw the maximum attention from the media, thus skewing our perception of a community. In each religious community, there are fringe voices and there are people who are working hard to initiate interfaith dialogue and to establish peace between different communal factions. These voices are never heard on prime-time news channels because voicing of moderate opinions seldom boosts their TRPs. On the contrary, sensationalizing issues help news channels sustain and/or increase their viewership and revenue earned from advertisements, sponsorships, partnerships and other forms of economic and political alliances. When children and adults consume media stories that sensationalize differences between religious communities, individuals start believing that their religion will ultimately decide their fate in the world. Constant exposure to and consumption of such biased media stories can influence children's everyday interactions with those from different religious communities.

When all that children can see and hear in their families, schools and media is discrimination and stereotyping, how will they find the resources to imagine a different reality?

Of course, the media has a great potential to present new possibilities and to enable individuals to reimagine ways of being in the world, but mainstream media companies are more driven by revenue generation than by democratic morals and values. If they make their audience uncomfortable, they risk losing their viewership and so they prefer to align their coverage with the dominant thoughts, practices and values in the society. When children consume media uncritically, they reproduce in their routines the aspirations and lifestyle choices projected by the media. This is how the media socializes children to behave within religious, gender, class and caste norms that benefit powerful groups in the society.

As we just discussed, families, schools and media are the three core dimensions in children's socialization. Recognizing these three dimensions as crucial sites where children learn most of their social behaviour is the starting point towards designing critical and inclusive experiences for them so that they can thrive in a diverse and multicultural world.

Adults can pay close attention to their personal biases as they educate and bring up children.

Religious and social biases are not merely mental concepts. They manifest in our language, behaviour and lived experiences. Let us look at the following flowchart to understand how bias is communicated, practised and experienced in our societies.

As the figure illustrates, bias thrives through practice, representation in media, cultural products such as songs, jokes and images, and circulation. The critical task of identifying the bias entails the massive project of 'unlearning'. Adults must be open to the idea of unlearning certain beliefs, values, attitudes

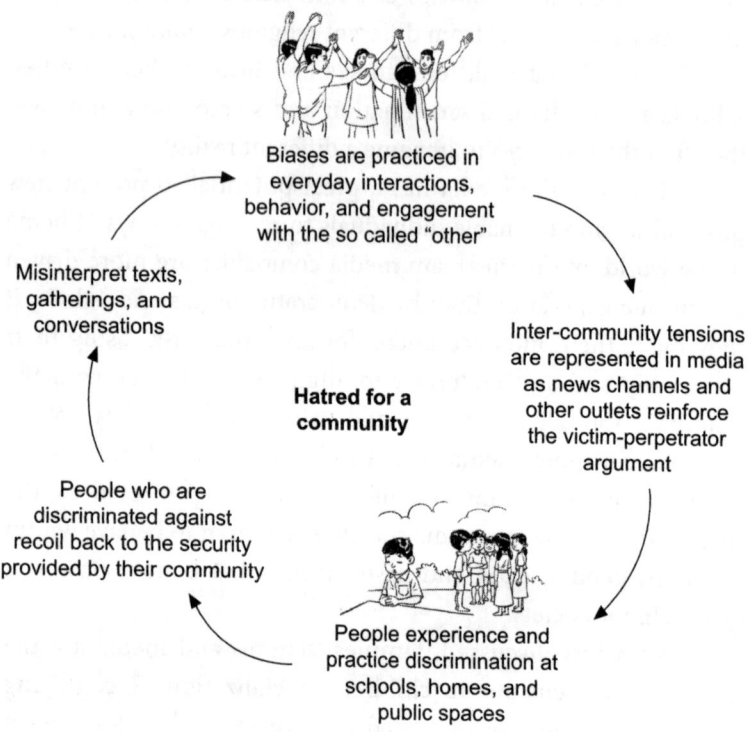

Biases are practiced in everyday interactions, behavior, and engagement with the so called "other"

Misinterpret texts, gatherings, and conversations

Inter-community tensions are represented in media as news channels and other outlets reinforce the victim-perpetrator argument

Hatred for a community

People who are discriminated against recoil back to the security provided by their community

People experience and practice discrimination at schools, homes, and public spaces

and practices if they want their children to be open to differences. Unlearning begins at homes and in schools where children can acknowledge their experiences of suffering and pain. It is an intimate and challenging undertaking in families and schools.

Raising children in such fractious times is a special kind of calling. It requires cultivating hope and investing a sense of joy and gratitude in our children so that they may be prepared to navigate through hatred, so that they have the strength to resist the pressures of conforming to unjust social norms. Before we begin the process of unlearning, it is important for us to examine what exactly we need to unlearn. That is what we do in the Chapter 2.

Echo Chambers
Our Seemingly Safe Cocoons

Who does not like a safe shelter that is comfortable and well insulated to keep the cold, heat, rain and wind at the bay? Heavy curtains shield its doors and windows. Only those we love are allowed inside. Anyone who makes us uncomfortable in the slightest way possible or gets into an argument is banished immediately. Our children will inherit these safe havens from us and live their lives in the same comforts that they are used to while growing up. Sounds wonderful, doesn't it? Well, we also have mental homes exactly like this, and you know what, there is nothing wonderful about it.

Communication scholars use various terms to describe these mental cocoons and the comfort we find there: echo chambers, silos and thought ghettos. All of these terms basically stand for a very common human behaviour: We like to stay in our mental, emotional and intellectual comfort zones. We like to hear, watch and read news, stories and ideas that support our own beliefs, opinions and ideologies, and we tend to shun ideas that challenge us and the people who question our tightly held beliefs.

ECHO CHAMBER

Echo chamber is a metaphor used to describe an environment where people surround themselves with others who think, feel and behave like them. In most cases, echo chambers are created when people choose to interact with those from the same religious, caste or class communities. Echo chambers are also created on the basis of age, geographical origin or certain expertise. It is easier for people to inhabit echo chambers because our immediate communities and in-group solidarity within these allow us to engage with people who have the same ideologies and belief systems. People actively choose to be part of such echo chambers because it makes them feel safe and certain about 'who they are' and 'what they believe in'. Let us take a look at the following diagram:

LET US INTROSPECT A LITTLE

Have you ever stopped your daughter from speaking up or questioning an unjust practice when it involves challenging an older male relative?

Have you ever experienced fear at the thought that your child may marry a person from a lower caste or a different religion or of the same sex?

Are you scared and heartbroken because your son shows inclination to study humanities instead of engineering?

And you are familiar with the constant buzz of *log kya kahenge* (what will people say) in our society, right?

Even before we are allowed to express who we are as individuals, our social identities establish the boundaries within which we are situated. These boundaries are the a priori filters through which others look at us and the way we experience the world. These filters are also responsible towards creating and sustaining stereotypes about others.

Also, did you observe something? Most of our echo chambers operate around gender, religion, caste and class. These four are the most important identities in a person's life and are at the base of our fears, suspicions, stereotypes and strong beliefs. These are predictors of what kind of treatment and bias a person will encounter in his or her life. It is therefore good to understand these four dimensions of our identity clearly at this point.

GENDER

WHAT IS THE DIFFERENCE BETWEEN GENDER AND SEX?

Many people use the words 'sex' and 'gender' interchangeably, but they do not mean the same thing. Sex is a term used to refer to the biological and physiological differences between males and females. The term 'sex' denotes physical differentiation between the bodies of men and women. That is the reason why infants are either categorized as girl or boy on the basis of these physical differentiations when they are born.

Gender, on the other hand, is a socially constructed concept that is used to assign roles, characteristics and lay down behavioural expectations from individuals on the basis of their sex. The differences in the roles of men and women or girls and boys are socially constructed and, in most cases, reinforce the patriarchal systems in our society. For ages, it was believed that the roles assigned to men and women were determined biologically and tied with the biological differences between them. In a way, women and their bodies were held responsible for their subordinate status in society. As this was naturalized in our societies, people found it easier to accept and make peace with the gender-based inequalities prevailing in our societies.

Over the years, many feminist scholars have argued against this, insisting that gender is a sociocultural concept and will therefore vary from one person to another and from one society to another. According to Ann Oakley, a leading feminist scholar, 'Gender is a matter of culture, it refers to the social classification of men and women into masculine and feminine roles.' This means that though sex is relatively constant, gender roles and expectations can be challenged, changed and modified.

If a woman can cook,
So can a man,
Because a woman doesn't cook with her womb.

—Kamla Bhasin

According to feminist-scholar Judith Butler,[1] gender identity is essentially a performance. Gender identity and the related roles assigned to people are 'compelled by social sanction and taboo'. Once we are labelled a boy or a girl, we are taught to constantly repeat our performance of that label through various daily acts sanctioned by our society—how we walk and talk, what we wear, who we befriend, what sports and hobbies we take up, what we are allowed to do or not allowed to do...it is an endless list. Sounds familiar?

Butler doesn't deny that physical differences exist, but she attempts to draw our attention to the ways in which some physical

---

[1] J. Butler, *Undoing Gender* (New York, NY: Routledge, 2004).

differences, such as the difference in genitals between people, come to acquire such significance that they define who they can be in our society. Interestingly, other physical differences, such as hair or eye colour, don't matter!

It is important to reflect on how our gender influences every aspect of our lives. Is there anything that remains unaffected by whether one is identified as a man or a woman or a transgender? Choices, education, romance, marriage, work, leisure, expectations and rewards, all of these get affected by the gender label that we carry. It is not always a matter of whether or not you feel constrained by your gender; it is the label that automatically decides many things, including how other people see and treat you.

LET US PAUSE AND THINK

Is it natural for women to be able to manage both home and paid work, or is it because women have been trained and conditioned to perform this dual role? Why cannot we train our men to participate in household chores? Why do we glorify the double burden—triple when there are kids and four times when there are elderly people in the family to care for—that women have to shoulder? This bias has affected women's health, career growth and well-being for generations. What are your observations?

We witness such patriarchal practices every day in our immediate family circles and environments. Patriarchy has a detrimental effect on the imagination of young boys and girls, as it severely restricts who they can be and what they can do. In creating rigid gender norms, patriarchy convinces people that those who challenge these norms are an aberration and must be disciplined. Patriarchy is toxic and violent at several levels. It limits imagination, punishes children for being creative about roles and rules, and creates unrealistic aspirations about body and self. It either reduces young people's bodies into a commodity for display and, through that, into a consumer of capital products, or it pressurizes them to modify their behaviour and bodies to match the dominant beauty ideals.

Gloria Steinem once said, 'We've begun to raise daughters more like sons, but few have the courage to raise our sons more like our daughters.' This raises some important questions: how can we persuade boys and men to challenge patriarchal tendencies both within themselves and within their communities? How can we advocate for a change in our families and communities so that young girls and boys can imagine ways to exist outside gender norms and thrive together?

How Many Genders Are There?

There is an interesting alternative idea; that is, gender is a spectrum. In other words, gender is no more a binary between men and women. Some people feel that the rigid gender expectations assigned to them at birth because of their sex and physical anatomy do not match the way they think and feel about themselves. Gender identity spectrum visualizes gender as a continuum stretching from men to women, masculine to feminine and boys to girls. This means that people can choose to be anywhere in this spectrum and to identify as possessing traits, feelings, emotions or conduct that is neither entirely male nor female. Looking at gender as a spectrum begins with acknowledging that gender is non-binary—it is much more than a simple categorization into male and female. For instance, some boys like to wear make-up and pay special attention to grooming and appearance. Some boys choose to be soft-spoken and demure, and still enjoy watching or participating in rough sports such as soccer. In fact, many of us are neither strictly masculine nor feminine, but we are forced to act as one. Gender identities are non-binary identities. Some mid-spectrum identities include the following:

> *Transgender:* A term used for people who do not identify with the gender associated with their sex and assigned to them at birth.
> *Agender:* A term used for people who do not identify with a gender.

Genderqueer or queer: A term people use when they feel that they are a confluence of or beyond the established gender identities.

LET US PAUSE AND THINK

Why are we assigned roles on the basis of our sex? Why do we think that if a person is a transgender, they are not suitable to perform the role of teacher, gardener, tailor, advertising manager or software engineer? How are these two completely unrelated dimensions—your sexual organs and vocational work—so conflated that we take this connection as natural? Do we realize that transgender people are forced out of work and livelihood options because of our biases?

Different Doesn't Mean Inferior or Superior

We know what some of us may be thinking right now. Aren't men and women biologically and psychologically different? Don't women need special attention when they are pregnant or nursing babies? Of course, yes. Men and women, however, do not have to be necessarily inferior or superior to each other. A mother certainly needs special privileges when she is nursing, and she should have them without any grudges, but that is about six months of her life. When it comes to feeding a child with a spoon, why do we insist that only the mother can do that? Do people need superpowers or some quality that only a woman possesses to change the diapers? If men can be super chefs, why can't they cook for the family?

These are just a few questions, but there are many such instances in our everyday lives where we must challenge our bias around gender and gender roles. Can you spot some more?

RELIGION

Let us do a small exercise. Can you think of a few residential societies in your cities where Hindus and Muslims share the same neighbourhood? Now, think how you would feel about buying a house in such a locality. What are your thoughts?

How would you respond to the following questions about buying a house in a neighbourhood dominated by people from a different religious community?

I will be very comfortable	Yes/No
I will be concerned about my family's safety	Yes/No
I will be concerned that property rates in such mixed neighbourhoods may fall over the years	Yes/No
I will be excited that my children/family members will get an opportunity to learn about a different religious community	Yes/No
I will be worried that my community will look down upon this decision	Yes/No
I will buy the house only if it is offered at a very cheap price	Yes/No
I will buy a house as an investment but would not stay there with my family	Yes/No
I will not buy a house in mixed neighbourhoods	Yes/No
Even if I want, the other community will not sell me the house	Yes/No

We understand that most people will experience a sense of scepticism inhabiting mixed neighbourhoods, given the history of communal conflicts in various parts of the country. We do not trivialize their fear because it is natural for people to worry about their own and their family's safety. What is truly noteworthy, however, is to recognize that in most cases we learn about people from other religions, not through personal interactions and experiences, but through indirect sources. Our understanding of the 'other' is informed by what we hear and see in our families, through the media, and in our peer circles. Very few of us have actually made an effort to question the filtered stories we have received and to challenge such one-sided perspectives through personal interactions and experiences with the 'other'.

This leads us to deliberate on some interesting questions on the influence of religion in our lives and its role in public and political spheres.

Religion in Public and at Home

Religion is a 'sacred canopy'; it protects people from uncertainty inherent in their lives. All religions in the world have something positive to teach their followers. It is, therefore, sad to witness that this institution is being used to create disharmony and hatred among communities. We have often observed how religion becomes an institution that manifests itself in public spaces such as temples, churches or mosques and how it changes from an intrapersonal, in-group experience to the staging of a public spectacle where our religion is pitted in contestation with other religions for gaining power. It is strange that practising one religion involves establishing how our religion is different and better than other religions.

The 'us, we, I' are pitted against the 'they and them'. These are called binaries. At the core of these binaries are feelings of discomfort, dislike and disdain for differences. Thinking in binaries creates absolute truths in isolation of context and experiences. Single truths provide us with a half-baked picture of reality. It is an easy practice because people do not have to invest in understanding how a single truth can play out differently in varied contexts.

This brings us to some very important questions: how can we unlearn our biases? For this, we must first understand the difference between beliefs and biases. When do your beliefs translate into acts of discrimination perpetuated against others?

From Religious Beliefs to Biases

People's religious identities have two dimensions: (a) belief and (b) practice/performance. Religious beliefs are practiced on a daily basis through rituals, clothing, food, lifestyle, intra/inter-community interactions and the organization of communities around a set of religious guidelines. Various facets of our daily lives reflect our religious identities. Our name, for instance, reveals our religious, caste and gender identities. This leads us to a very important question: what are religious stereotypes, and how do they lead to religious discrimination?

Stereotypes are either based on common behavioural practices observed in a community and reinforced by media and social listening, or some historical events connected to the community. For instance, the partition of India in 1947 resulted in major communal violence between Hindus and Muslims across borders and in other parts of the country. The memory of the partition—the lives lost and the families separated—has left an indelible mark on the very sociopolitical fabric of the country. Both Hindu and Muslim communities in India continue to hold each other responsible for the violence in 1947. The memory of a single devastating event, the partition in 1947, strained Hindu–Muslims relations forever. Although we like to believe that the memory of this event is dying, gradually fading into a chapter from our history texts, the truth remains that this event continues to shape how Hindus and Muslims perceive and relate to each other. Hatred and bias originating from the memory of this event is strengthened by narratives about each community. Muslims are commonly referred to as *kattar*, that is, rigid/conservatives/fanatics who intend to proselytize everyone and convert all to Islam. On the other hand, Hindus are portrayed as perpetrators who continue to violate Muslims and refuse them their rights. Such single stories are responsible for the many harmful narratives that continue to plague our societies. Similarly, the memory of India's colonial encounters with Christianity and the religious ambitions of the Britishers to proselytize people in the Indian subcontinent and promote monotheism has established the Christian community as the antagonist to traditions of indigenous groups in India who worship multiple deities. Several conflicts between different religious communities in India are foregrounded in such historical events. There are two problems here: one, very few of us have studied history in detail and with a critical lens. Besides, every historical event has multiple versions depending on who is narrating it and for what purpose. If we are not vigilant, we may fall prey to half-baked and exaggerated stories. Let us consider how WhatsApp has now become a major history instructor! Second, we forget that carrying this historical baggage in the changed times is going to hurt rather than help communities. Although we agree that painful memories are hard to forget and experiences of injustice are carried forward, affecting generations after generations, it is critical to challenge this attitude.

To reorient our thinking, let us consider the fact that religion is often used as a political tool and has become a number game. People are often hesitant to admit that there is strength in numbers, that is, the larger the congregation, the more power it wields over available resources and territories. Eventually, the community with the largest followers enjoys complete control over social, economic, cultural and political resources. It is this conceptualization of religion that helps us to understand why religious communities are in perpetual conflict with each other. For instance, many religious texts encourage their followers to discriminate between believers and non-believers (including believers of other religions). Fostering such a tense and antagonistic relationship between the self and the other makes it very difficult to imagine ways to challenge our toxic approach towards the other. We can change our toxic relations only if all religions equally participate in the process of accepting differences.

LET US PAUSE AND THINK!

Do you spot the connection between religion and gender here?

Love Jihad is a negative term that has entered our vocabulary in the past decade. It means a Muslim man marrying a Hindu woman. It never means a Muslim woman marrying a Hindu man. Why?

Here is where patriarchy (the male-dominated nature of society) enters. In patriarchal societies, including ours, the community to which the man belongs gains membership when a man brings home a bride, while the community to which a woman belongs is supposed to lose one. This is because traditionally after marriage, a woman is no more considered a part of her biological family. Sad, isn't it? Of course, resentment is equal in a Muslim community when a Muslim woman marries a Hindu man.

Shouldn't both communities see it as getting a new member?

CASTE

How Does the Caste System Affect Our Children and Societies?

Payal Tadvi,[2] a 26-year-old medical student, was bullied and harassed by her seniors at Topiwala National Medical College and the BYL Nair Hospital because of her low-caste identity. On May 22 2019, Payal committed suicide.

---

[2] M. Sadaf, 'Payal Tadvi Suicide Case: "Work Out Practical Solution on Plea Filed by Accused Seeking to Resume Study"', *The Indian Express* (2020). Available at https://indianexpress.com/article/india/payal-tadvi-suicide-case-work-out-practical-solution-on-plea-filed-by-accused-seeking-to-resume-study-6243369/ (accessed on 9 April 2020).

Nitin Aage,[3] a 17-year-old boy from a village called Kharda, was found hanging from a tree on 28 April 2014. According to the police, Nitin had been seen speaking to a girl from an upper caste community at their school. Three men, including the girl's brother, allegedly harassed him for some time because they suspected that he was in a romantic relationship with her.

Ten-year-old Rajashree Kamble[4] hurt herself on the head when she slipped and fell while fetching water. Her father, Namdev, alleges that his daughter would be alive if the Dalit neighbourhood where they lived had received their daily supply of water.

In 2016, there was a major uprising and revolt staged by members of the Dalit community when seven members of a Dalit family near Una, Gujarat, were flogged by upper caste cow-vigilant group for doing their job, that is, skinning the carcasses of a dead cow. They were beaten, flogged publicly and tortured because of their profession and caste identities. There have also been incidents of Dalit youth punished for indulging in everyday practices normalized as privileges granted exclusively to the upper castes, such as sporting a moustache or riding a horse for a wedding procession. Our schools, universities, offices and other public spaces are replete with such instances of caste-based violence.

India is changing rapidly, but it continues to uphold the regressive clutches of the caste system. It is tempting to believe that the caste system is nothing but a way of organizing society based on the work that people do. There is also evidence that caste groups have provided people with social support and a sense of belonging.

---

[3] A. Byatnal, 'I Had Told My Son to Stay Away from Maratha Girl, Says Slain Dalit's Mother', *The Hindu* (2014). Available at https://www.thehindu.com/news/national/other-states/i-had-told-my-son-to-stay-away-from-maratha-girl-says-slain-dalits-mother/article5963722.ece (accessed on 9 April 2020).

[4] S. Ghagte and S. Olwe, 'Shackled by Caste', *Fountainink* (2017). Available at https://fountainink.in/story/shackled-by-caste/ (accessed on 9 April 2020).

Well, these benign functions, however, hide a system of violent and hierarchical categorization of people that has been in place for generations and centuries. People who are at a lower level in this hierarchy are called lower castes. They have suffered and continue to experience systemic marginalization and discrimination in their daily lives. Do you know about the breast tax?

The Breast Tax: From Then to Now

THE BREAST TAX

'Breast tax' was a system imposed on lower-caste women in the erstwhile princely state of Travancore. Women from the lower castes were forced to pay a tax if they wanted to cover their breasts in public. The king's officials would visit the lower-caste neighbourhoods, examine the breasts of women with their bare hands and tax them on the weight and size of their breasts.

In 1803, Nangeli, a lower-caste Ezhava woman from the Nader community refused to pay the tax in defiance of this discriminatory law. When senior tax officials heard of this dissent, they sent a tax collector to her house to compel her to pay tax. Instead of complying with the tax collector, Nangeli cut off her breasts and offered them as a present to the collector. Nangeli succumbed to her injuries, but her act of defiance forced the king to withdraw the breast tax from Nader.

This system was essentially designed to reinforce the then existing dehumanization and oppression of lower castes in Travancore and afforded the right to dignity only to higher caste women. In his book, *Native Life in Travancore*, writer Samuel Mateer enlists 110 other taxes which were imposed primarily on people from the lower caste to reify the old traditions and caste hierarchy in society.

There are conscious efforts being made to raise awareness, delegitimize the caste system and grant everyone equal access to opportunities in life. These systems of change, however, have proven inefficient to alleviate caste-based discrimination because they are so deeply entrenched in our upbringing. Even today, when parents and families arrange a matrimony for their children, they insist that prospective partners are from their caste. We have met so many educated urban elites who would insist on marrying someone from their caste and have serious reservations against marrying those from a lower caste.

TO LAUGH OR CRY?

Sometime in the future...

Rahul: Mom, I want to marry Shankar.

Mother: That is not possible.

Rahul: But mom, gay marriage is now legal in India.

Mother: But he is not from our caste.

THE SEED HAS FORMED ROOTS

Jasmeen works for a software giant in the USA.

She eats lunch at the company's cafeteria. Once she joined a group of engineers of Indian origin working for the same company. A couple of them were second-generation NRIs. As they were eating their lunch and chatting away, another engineer of Indian origin walked to their table with his plate. The second-generation engineers looked at him with unease, obviously not happy at his joining the group. After a while, they got up on the pretext of refilling their plates and never returned to the table.

It was only later that Jasmeen found out that the new joiner was from a so-called lower caste in India, and that the two-second generation NRIs who left were socialized into believing that you could not eat or share food with a lower-caste person.

LET US PAUSE AND THINK

What do our children observe?

1. We identify people as lower caste on the basis of their surnames, and we use abuses such as *bhangi*, *chuda*, *chamar* and several other casteist slurs.
2. We call the people who come to collect garbage as *kachrewali*. Instead of familiarizing ourselves with their names, we reduce them to the labour they do. When you refuse to recognize a person as an individual, you invisibilize them and make them look insignificant.
3. We do not allow our children to befriend their classmates from a lower caste.
4. Lower-caste and Dalit students seldom share their lunch boxes/meals with students from the high caste.
5. People do not hire lower-caste women as cooks for their families.
6. Dalits and other lower-caste members are still not allowed to enter several places of worship in the country.
7. We barely pay attention to the inhuman practice of manual scavenging and the tragedy of workers doing this job; we rarely contribute to changing this practice, but we do stigmatize them for the work they are forced into.

Many upper caste people are now protesting against caste-based reservations. Well, we cannot deny that there are some issues, such as some wealthy members from the lower castes appropriating these benefits, or some genuinely bright students from poor upper caste families losing opportunities, or no visible long-term change in the relations between castes. However, when people argue for merit-based opportunities, they completely ignore the role their wealth, social networks and connections play in acquiring merit! We certainly need a more innovative and fair solution.

CLASS

By class, we mean economic class. When we belong to a financially comfortable upper class, we see many things as normal. We also see these things as our right, our entitlement. We convince ourselves that we and our children should enjoy certain privileges, because it is through sheer hard work that we have earned this money. This may be partially true but there is a catch here. Are all the people who are not as rich as we are poor because of laziness? Are there any other factors that keep people poor? Should we look down upon people because they have less money than us, even though they may have all the other qualities of a good human being? Should we maintain a complete distance from those who are not in the same financial league as us?

HOW DOES THE CLASS SYSTEM WORK?

It does take individual qualities such as positive attitude, belief, hard work, intelligence, acumen and aspiration for a person to succeed. There is no question about it. Negative individual life conditions can keep people poor—low education, unwillingness to work hard, lack of motivation and lack of competency are some of these factors.

We suggest you think again. Isn't it easier to get education and competency when we have the money to acquire them? Why are some jobs so low-paying that, after working for an entire day or even doing double shifts, people do not make enough money to give their children good food and education? For example, why are nannies paid so poorly when our children are our most valuable assets? The COVID-19-induced lockdown brought many of us down to our knees when we had to do all the cleaning ourselves. Did we question why household help is paid so less for such arduous work? Somehow, these poor salaries have become an established norm; we follow these norms unquestioningly. Many hard-working families continue to suffer in poverty and cannot break the cycle of low education, poor health, lack of sanitary resources and harmful social practices.

So individual qualities are important in acquiring wealth, but ethical and humane practices are equally important in keeping families in comfortable economic conditions. How can we contribute to this?

Let's take a little test. List all the people whose presence in your life you missed most strongly during the lockdown. Now list how much they are paid. Do you see an inverse relationship? We pay the least to our garbage collectors, cleaners and maintenance people, but their services are the most essential in running our lives smoothly!

Overlaps in Our Identities

Our identities have multiple dimensions and we sometimes face prejudice because of our age, skin colour, geographical origin, education, profession, physical abilities, language, among others. Sometimes an individual receives benefits because of these, and sometimes they face discrimination. The real issue at the heart of this problem is that we are reducing a complex human being to a single dimension and deciding our behaviour and our treatment of this person simply on the basis of this one facet of their identity.

Now let us explore some episodes from our collective past to understand how gender, religion, caste and class are vectors around which violence is enacted. In 1989, Kashmiri pandits were forced out of their homes in the Kashmir valley and have been living in exile ever since. The communal riots between Hindus and Muslims in Gujarat in 2002 led to large-scale killings, rapes and loot. In 2012, a young girl was brutally gang raped and violated by six men on a moving bus in Delhi. In 2014, two teenage girls from the Other Backward Castes in the Katra village of Badaun district, Uttar Pradesh, were gang raped and murdered by high-caste men. These are a few cases of violence that received widespread media coverage, but many such incidents happen across the country every day. In all these instances, many people were brutalized only on the basis of their gender, religion or caste.

Intercommunal conflicts, the all-pervasiveness of patriarchy in Indian society, violence against girls and women, and discrimination facing the lower caste communities in India may appear as instances far removed from our cocooned lives, but we often play a part—many a time unknowingly—in perpetuating and reinforcing these problems through our everyday interactions.

Your beliefs become your thoughts,

Your thoughts become your words,

Your words become your actions,

Your actions become your habits,

Your habits become your values,

Your values become your destiny.

—Mahatma Gandhi

We are all interconnected in a web of exchange. We share resources, capital and spaces with others. If children are socialized to identify differences as inherently evil, they will be unable to thrive in a pluralistic society. Also, refusing to accept the discontinuities in one's own thinking may result in people discriminating against or dominating others. Every form of discrimination and violence can escalate into societal conflicts and disturb the very fabric of our societies. In some extreme situations, refusing to step out of our echo chambers may lead to an unfathomable divide between different communities, often resulting in irreconcilable segregations, both physical and ideological. All this disturbs the harmony of everyday living.

Though there are laws to protect people from discrimination on the basis of caste and gender, provisions to protect religious minorities and acts such as the right to education that protects the educational rights of poor children, unless individuals change their actions and behaviour, a lasting social change is not possible. Also, many a times, the oppressed communities become oppressors. They may cultivate a closed mindset and be prejudiced against the other. On the contrary, there are several instances of community action—be it a country, a city, an institution or an organization, where communities have welcomed others, offered hospitality and willingly shared resources. So we all have to unlearn and learn together. We will discuss how to open our hearts and minds, and unlearn together in the chapters that follow.

CHAPTER 3

Tolerance
Philosophies and Principles

हिन्दू की दया, मेहर तुरकन की, दोनों घर से भागी,
वह करै जिभह, वो झटका मारै, आगि दुओ घर लागी।

हिन्दू कहत है, राम हमारा, मुसलमान रह्याना,
आपस में दोउ लड़े मरत हैं, भेद न कोई जाना।[1]

कबीर

Our field visits have taken us to different cities and towns of
India—from the small villages of Telav and Ghuma in Gujarat to
the sprawling cities of Delhi and Mumbai. All our visits have led us
to believe that the virtue of tolerance and compassion is woven into
the very fabric of our Indian society. Even when periods of inva-
sion and violence disrupted the harmony of our society and when
discriminatory beliefs and practices threatened the well-being of
vulnerable groups, there have always been attempts by thinkers,
leaders, artists and many citizens to restore peaceful coexistence.
During one such research trip, we spent considerable time at
Jama Masjid, the oldest mosque in Ahmedabad, and observed
that despite the conflict-ridden history of the two communities,
the place was revered by both Muslim and Hindu visitors. From
a historical perspective, this monument houses the mosque of
Ahmad Shah, and its construction bears witness to the synthesis
of both Hindu and Jain styles of architecture. In the present times,
this structure embraces visitors-believers and non-believers,
from different faith backgrounds, and we could see people from
different religions praying at the *dargah*, contemplating the style
and architecture of the Jamatkhana or watching the sunset from
the balcony.

Another example of the composite culture of the city is the
Gandhi Ashram, built on the banks of the Sabarmati river—a critical

---

[1] Translation: Hindu's mercy and Muslim's benevolence, both left the house; one practices
Halal, while the other practices *Jhatka*, and there was fire on both sides.
Hindu says that Ram is ours, for the Muslims it is Rahim, they both die fighting each other,
but neither knows the difference between both of them.

site for forging the national freedom movement in the pre-1947 era. This city and the ashram became a place for Mahatma Gandhi's experiments with truth and non-violence; he initiated many freedom movements, including the Dandi March, from this ashram. The city also stood as a testimony to the national efforts of Sardar Vallabhbhai Patel towards forging alliances with different states, communities and kingdoms to challenge colonial powers and create a nation state.

These stories restore our hope that we can still shape the cities and villages we love to call our homes on the practices of tolerance and coexistence. Today, cities that emerged as sites of unified national movements have witnessed tragic instances of communal, caste-based, gender-based and other forms of violence. In Ahmedabad, for instance, since 1967, several communal conflicts between Hindus and Muslims have ruined interfaith relations in the city.[2] Residential housings and societies in the city, for instance, are segregated on the basis of religion such that Muslims and Hindus stay separately and in clearly demarcated areas of the city.[3]

Given a choice, we all would want our children to live in places where they are safe and are able to thrive, regardless of gender, caste or religion. Well, we can build such places only if we contribute to uphold and promote harmony in our societies. For this, some leaders advocate celebrating and embracing differences, some advise accepting differences, and if we cannot do either of these things, the least we can do is practise tolerance.

Many scholars have questioned the use of the word 'tolerance' which implies that tolerance may or may not include acceptance. The phrase 'I tolerate them' has a negative connotation because, here, the word 'tolerate' is spoken as an obligation towards the laws/rules of the country or society. For instance, when we use

[2] N. Sud, *Liberalization, Hindu Nationalism, and the State: A Biography of Gujarat* (New York, NY: Oxford University Press, 2010).

[3] K. Bhatia and M. Pathak-Shelat, 'Reimagining Religiously Segregated Spaces: Building Interfaith Sites through Participatory Photography', *Journal of Communication Inquiry* (2020). 10.1177/0196859920918543.

the phrase 'we tolerate lower caste people', we articulate a sense of compulsion rather than acceptance, that is, a situation enforced onto us because our constitution criminalizes any discrimination on the basis of caste. We, however, wish to argue that this is a rather narrow and colloquially generated meaning of the word. The noun 'tolerance' encompasses much more than the act of 'tolerating the other'. Tolerance is a *process* of creating a space for the most uncomfortable, divergent or radically different ideas to thrive. Tolerance is an *ideal* wedded with compassionate practices, and it allows people to experience sympathy towards those who are very different from us. Tolerance involves accepting the faults in our own thinking and our understanding of the world. To be tolerant is to start from a place of self-doubt and acknowledge that whatever we think and/or believe is only a partial approximation of the truth. At the very least, tolerance is 'never causing harm to others', physically or emotionally, just because they think and behave differently from us. Tolerance involves putting up with some discomfort.

Intolerance begins with small things, and it is not simple to differentiate between personal preferences/likes–dislikes and our deeper core values.

LET US PAUSE AND THINK!

Suppose you are vegetarian, and you cannot bear the smell from cooking fish. It is natural that having a neighbour who cooks fish every day is bound to cause genuine unease.

Suppose you hate dogs and are also allergic to them, but there are people in your society who treat their dogs like their children.

Suppose you have been brought up in a strictly heterosexual ideology, and you find it difficult to accept gay couples. Your nephew has a partner who is a man, and the couple is present at several family functions.

What rights do you have to preserve your way of life and preferences, and when should you let go to respect others?

Is some discomfort reason enough for you to shut them off and keep them away? Worse, given a chance, would you attack them verbally or physically?

In the following sections, we explain why the practice of tolerance is critical for the health of both our Indian democracy and its rich culture. We also draw from world leaders who time and again reminded us to follow peaceful coexistence amid our very real differences.

TOLERANCE IS AMICABLE COEXISTENCE

Unlike what many people think, tolerance is not an indifference towards or a refusal to engage with others. In today's world, with long histories of travel, migration and intermingling of people, can we imagine any community living in complete isolation? Are the regressive and mythical ideas of purity, pollution and fear of contamination from other cultures really valid?

Every day, each one of us enters into multiple transactions in schools, offices, streets, public spaces, entertainment sites and so on. Our children go to schools and have the opportunity of befriending others who have different belief systems and lifestyles. Similarly, at work, we have colleagues from diverse social backgrounds who bring new perspectives and insights into our office spaces. We learn about people, projects and places that speak to the diversity inherent in our culture and societies.

Ideas of purity and pollution draw strength from a belief that we can reach or possess an absolute truth; they are nestled in a refusal to question the partiality of our own beliefs and opinions. According to Gandhi,[4] every person is inclined to believe that there is an absolute truth in the world, and this truth proves to be

---

[4] M. K. Gandhi, *My Non-violence* (Ahmedabad: Navajivan Mudranalaya, 1960). Available at https://www.mkgandhi.org/mynonviolence/my_nonviolence.htm (accessed on 28 October 2020).

a blanket for people in times of uncertainty such as death, disease, famine or a global pandemic. This precondition for proclaiming one's truth as absolute is the cause of intolerance in our societies.

> There is no story that is not true. The world has no end, and what is good among one people is an abomination with others.
>
> —Chinua Achebe in *Things Fall Apart*

Gandhi[5] explains:

I have been striving to search for the truth and have the courage to jump from the Himalayas for its sake. But, I know I am still far from that truth. As I advance towards it, I perceive my weakness ever more clearly and the knowledge makes me humble.

Teachings of Gandhi encourage us to debunk the notion that anyone can possess absolute truth and, by that logic, occupy a position superior to others. Each one of us has the freedom and the moral spectrum to seek our own truths, but these quests can never culminate into a universal moral code. The practice of tolerance encourages people to question the belief that their life choices are universally good and that there is only one right way of doing everything—eating, raising children, practising religion or expressing love.

Gandhi, the father of our nation, wanted to create a *Swaraj*, the rule of people, in India. Gandhi's *Swaraj* was an ideal based on the principles of tolerance and equality, where every person could claim and enjoy a stake in the nation-building process. Gandhi[6] explains, 'At the individual level swaraj is vitally connected

---

[5] M. K. Gandhi, *An Autobiography: The Story of my Experiments with Truth* (New York, NY: Dover Publications, 1927).

[6] M. K. Gandhi, *Hind Swaraj* (Ahmedabad: Navajivan Mudranalaya, 1909).

with the capacity for dispassionate self-assessment, ceaseless self-purification, and growing self-reliance.' The three tenets of *Swaraj* are all closely linked with the conscientious practices of critically questioning the merits, challenges, limitations and evils of our partial truths. For a practising devout Christian, this process may involve asking questions related to the oppression inbuilt in the act of proselytizing masses—a phenomenon witnessed by many previously colonized regions in the Indian subcontinent, the continent of Africa, China, Japan and other places. The colonial project was designed around the religious doctrine of proselytization and led to mass violence and oppression. The historicity of our colonial past weighs heavily on our present as we think about the several Western imports that have turned religion into a public spectacle and a tool for dividing the populace. Similarly, the caste system in the Hindu religion is responsible for the continued and systemic marginalization and subjugation of caste minorities. Hindus should be willing to denounce the caste system and create just and more inclusive ways of organizing themselves in their communities. Muslims need to ask why anyone who refuses to accept Islam as the only true religion should be labelled a kafir and should be a target of hatred. What is more interesting is that even within every religion, there are so many ways of creating 'us and them' boundaries—Catholics and Protestants, Shaivites and Vaishnavites, Shias and Sunnis! And then there are atheists who ridicule everyone else and everyone else looks at them with suspicion!

Once we get into the habit of creating walls, it is never ending.

TOLERANCE (IN TRUTH IS GOD)

M. K. GANDHI

The question then arises: Why should there be so many faiths? We know that there are a large variety of them. The soul is one, but the bodies which she animates are many. We cannot reduce the number of bodies, yet we recognize the unity of the soul. Even as a tree has a single trunk, but many branches and leaves, there is one religion, but any number of faiths. All faiths are a gift of God, but partake of human imperfection, as they pass through the medium of humanity. God-given religion is beyond all speech. Imperfect men put it into such language as they can command, and their words are interpreted by other men equally imperfect. Whose interpretation must be held to be the right one? Everyone is right from his own standpoint, but it is not impossible that everyone is wrong. Hence, the necessity for tolerance, which does not mean indifference towards one's own faith, but more intelligent and purer love for it. Tolerance gives us a spiritual insight that is as far from fanaticism as the North Pole is from the South. True knowledge of religion breaks down the barriers between faith and faith, giving rise to tolerance. Cultivation of tolerance for other faiths will impart to us a truer understanding of our own.

Gandhi borrowed heavily from Western scholars and thinkers such as Socrates, Locke and Kant. In the following section, we visit the works of some of these scholars who had an influence on Gandhi and/or can inform the practice of tolerance in India.

LIVING WITH DIFFERENCES

Gandhi's ideas of truth and tolerance borrow from the Socratic traditions of subjecting one's truths to a rigorous scrutiny to prevent us from participating in myths and fantasies of hate, prejudice, bias and violence. This practice of scrutinizing our own opinions of others can prevent us from falling prey to stereotyping others.

For instance, representations of Muslims in the media are extremely stereotypical. A Muslim character is either projected as a perpetrator of violence—a terrorist, criminal or a murderer, or is presented as a victim who faces immense discrimination. In either case, the Muslim character is restricted to the 'perpetrator-victim' binary and this limits people from realistically imagining alternate ways of perceiving Muslims. Similarly, the way Hinduism is articulated in Western media today may lead people to look at every Hindu as a sword-brandishing fanatic.

Tolerance pushes people to transcend their boundaries and engage with the question, who is a Muslim? Or who is a Hindu? from a fresh perspective, using new sources of opinion formation.

Tolerance is strengthened by the philosophical virtue of doubt. Cultivating a sense of doubt may sound negative, but it can prove to be beneficial. Let us revisit a tale from the Mahabharata where a Brahmin learns about tolerance and non-violence.

Kaushika had mastered spiritual studies and was sitting under a tree in penance when he was distracted by a bird on the tree. In his anger, he uses his powers to turn the innocent bird into ashes with his gaze. He immediately realizes how his mastery of spiritual studies was morally decrepit because he was oppressing, violating and causing harm to others with his power. His transformation began when he accepted that his knowledge was limited, and his truth was not universal. He began to realize that some of the truths he possessed and held so dear were merely assumptions about himself and the world. His mind was inflicted with self-doubt—doubt about his mastery over spiritual studies and practices, about the ethicality of his actions and about the all-encompassing power of his truth. A sense of doubt made him acknowledge his imperfections and seek guidance and counsel.

In the absence of tolerance, countries have witnessed un-precedented violence, and this has tarnished the moral fabric of societies, destroyed communities and led to mass scale killings. Violent history of slavery in several countries, anti-Semitism and the Holocaust in Germany and other states in Europe, violence against LGBTQIA people, racial lynching in the USA, the mass execution and displacement of Rohingyas in Myanmar, the bloodshed during the India–Pakistan partition and the continued oppression of religious minorities in China have all left an indelible mark on intergroup relations and the functioning of societies. Many peace leaders across the globe have used tolerance and compassion as a strategy to fight injustice and violence. Let us look at the teachings of some world leaders and artists who promoted the ideals of tolerance and non-violence in their work, policies and conduct.

Nelson Mandela was an anti-apartheid revolutionary in South Africa who spent 27 years in prison for demanding racial justice and equality. Throughout his journey as a political leader and a social activist, Mandela emphasized forgiveness. He focused on the process of reconciling differences. Mandela spent years in prison. Can we imagine being able to forgive those who caused so much pain and suffering? But he did. Historical wrongs can be righted, he argued, only when people are ready to forgive their oppressors and imagine a future where this binary between victim and perpetrators can be undone. Democracy depends on a fine balance between freedom and tolerance. People should have the freedom to express their opinions, to enact their identities and to aspire without fear, but they should also be willing to respond to other people's ideas and opinions with sensitivity and tolerance. Tolerance, therefore, is our ethical responsibility enacted in lieu of being able to experience freedom and liberty.

> Bridge the chasm, use tolerance and compassion, be inclusive not exclusive, build dignity and pride, encourage freedom of expression to create a civil society for unity and peace.

> —Nelson Mandela

Tenzin Gyatso, the 14th Dalai Lama, is a champion of peace, tolerance and non-violence in the world. He fled his homeland during the Tibetan uprisings in 1959 and has been living as a refugee in India. Since then, he has travelled across the world and has promoted religious tolerance, compassion and peace. According to him, tolerance requires developing a scepticism about our religious beliefs and opinions of the world. It is a process of training 'the self' to rigorously analyse all truth—statements we encounter in our lives and corroborating these with empirical facts and information. Unlike Gandhi and other scholars who argue that there is no universal truth, the Dalai Lama explains that 'humanity' is the single truth that connects everyone and transcends differences in religion, class, caste, gender and other social distinctions. Our belief in, or our search to establish humanism as the singular and universal truth, creates a comparative logic wherein one community is pitted against the other. Conflicts and violence, according to the Dalai Lama, are the outcomes of ill-conceived notions of acquiring power and ascendancy. The existence of our world, our planet and our lives is anchored onto a serene balance of differences and similarities. Tolerances towards differences and collaboration through similarities makes the conditions for peaceful coexistence possible.

According to him, our obligation towards protecting 'the humane' in our societies must precede our narrower commitments towards our personal social identities. Tolerance involves accountability for all of our actions, words and thoughts, and analysing how they affect others.

Compassion, tolerance, forgiveness and a sense of self-discipline are qualities that help us lead our daily lives with a calm mind.

—Dalai Lama

Martin Luther King Jr. was a very influential leader of the Civil Rights Movement in the USA and practised non-violence, tolerance and civil disobedience in his fight for racial justice and equality. In his Nobel Peace Prize speech, he advanced the notions of tolerance and non-violence to sustain the creation of a just society. According to him, countries and people who refuse to practise tolerance in their political struggles often resort to violence and hatred. A violent strategy may help a country succeed temporarily on the battle ground, but it always fails to resolve internal social problems such as ethnic prejudice, communal hate and intergroup conflicts. The method of tolerance is a life-enriching force that ends the cycle of violence and revenge. On the contrary, intolerance renders all channels to create shared spaces of experience and conversations inaccessible, and thus reinforces the prevailing animosity among groups.

We will not build a peaceful world by following a negative path. It is not enough to say, 'We must not wage war.' It is necessary to love peace and sacrifice for it. We must concentrate not merely on the negative expulsion of war, but on the positive affirmation of peace.

—Martin Luther King Jr.

Wangari Maathai is the first African woman to have won the Nobel Peace Prize. For years, she has worked to promote women's rights and environmental conservation in Kenya and other parts of the world. She advocates empowerment for women and involves women in the process of planting trees and conserving the environment. In an interview with Krista Tippett,[7] she explained that a feminist approach towards social issues is essentially built on ideas of tolerance and peace. Unlike the dominant patriarchal society that creates oppressive hierarchies and deems some people, gender, class, community, words and conduct as unacceptable, a feminist movement, such as the one led by Maathai, emphasizes on generating safe, non-hierarchical spaces where profound disagreements between people can cohabit. This does not mean that all radically different ideas can be assimilated into one shared ideology. Feminism, she argues, is an attempt to stretch the fabric of our society to ensure that these unassimilable ideas can thrive without the threat of being erased, punished or ignored. For her, conflicts arise from human follies—prejudice, hate and greed.

---

[7] M. Wangari, 'Marching with Trees'. On Being with Krista Tippett (2018). Available at https://onbeing.org/programs/wangari-maathai-marching-with-trees/ (accessed on 28 October 2020).

We often forget that nature is the common thread that binds us all, and so practising tolerance in our lives requires us to look for 'God' not in people or places, but out there in the natural world. Tolerance and peace, for her, means designing sustainable ways to coexist with nature.

Now, where is God? And I tell myself, of course, now we are in a completely new era when we are learning to find God not in a place but rather in ourselves, in each other, in nature. In many ways, it's a contradiction because the church teaches you that God is omnipresent. Now, if he is omnipresent, he is in Rome, but he can also be in Kenya at the same time, if he is omnipresent.

So I have had this transformation for me of who God is. I still believe strongly that there is that power. His shape, his size, his colour, I have no idea. When I look at Mount Kenya, it is so magnificent, it is so overpowering.... It is so important in sustaining life in my area that sometimes I say, yes, God is on this mountain.

—Wangari Maathai

Tawakkol Karman is a Yemeni Nobel Laureate, journalist, peace activist and politician. According to her, tolerance is a political virtue, the bedrock of a democratic society. Tolerance in politically turbulent times means drafting and following common, shared guidelines for public dialogue and action. A tolerant society strives to ensure that every voice finds a representation in the nation-building process, that everyone is bound by the moral principles of equality for all, regardless of their social identities or beliefs and that people rely on consensus building, deliberation and dialogues. Tolerance is the process of prioritizing the common good, shared interest and public well-being over self-gain, private profits or personal opinions.

When I heard the news that I had got the Nobel Peace Prize, I was in my tent in the Taghyeer square in Sana'a. I was one of millions of revolutionary youth. There, we were not even able to secure our safety from the repression  and oppression of the regime of Ali Abdullah Saleh. At that moment, I contemplated the distinction between the meanings of peace and tolerance celebrated by the Nobel Prize, and the tragedy of the aggression waged by Ali Abdullah Saleh against the forces of peaceful change. However, our joy of being on the right side of history made it easier for us to bear the devastating irony.

Millions of Yemeni women and men, children, young and old took to the streets in 18 provinces demanding their right to freedom, justice and dignity, using non-violent but effective means to achieve their demands. We were able to efficiently and effectively maintain a peaceful revolution in spite of the fact that this great nation has more than 70 million firearms of various types. Here lies the philosophy of a tolerant revolution, which persuaded millions of people to leave their weapons at home and join the peaceful march against the state's machine of murder and violence, just with flowers and bare breasts, and filled with dreams, love and peace. We were very happy because we realized, at that time, that the Nobel Prize did not come only as a personal prize for Tawakkol Abdel-Salam Karman, but as a declaration and recognition of the whole world for the triumph of the peaceful revolution of Yemen and as an appreciation of the sacrifices of its great peaceful people.

—Tawakkol Karman

According to all these world leaders, tolerance is a civic virtue that compels people to evaluate their opinions, religious belief, political ideology and everyday practices with seasoned scepticism. Differences in our societies can be in conversations with each other without being at war. Tolerance, in our contemporary societies, can be defined as IDEA:

- Identifying the historical roots of the prevailing difference
- Defining common goals, shared interests and aspirations
- Eliminating violent impulses and substituting them with participatory and democratic practices rooted in the ideals of justice and empathy
- Acknowledging the tensions in our societies due to unassimilable differences and negotiating with them through public dialogue, deliberation and debates

India is a vast and pluralistic country, and it will always be home to people of different beliefs in every aspect of life. These beliefs will sometimes appear to be irrational, yet people are sentimental and emotional about them. Conflicts arise when these irrational cultural and religious beliefs clash with progressive civic goals. People will continue to hold some of these irrational beliefs or rituals, but it is important to establish the private–public distinction so that people do not establish their own beliefs as societal standards and force others to adopt and practise them. Tolerance is learning the boundaries of public–private, and while we may continue to perform certain rituals in our homes and in our personal lives, the public should be governed and regulated according to shared civic goals and liberties. In the following section, we will look at some examples of coexistence and consensus building in India.

PHILOSOPHIES AND TRADITIONS: LESSONS ON COEXISTENCE FROM INDIA

The Indian subcontinent has produced competing philosophies, ideologies and practices, and signals a tradition in synthetic approach. According to this approach, new ideas are continuously added to the existing system of thoughts without trivializing old ideas. Let us look at the story of the arrival of the Zoroastrian community in India.

Sometime in the 10th century, a small group of Parsees or Zoroastrians fled the execution in Persia and reached Gujarat. When they petitioned King Jadav to provide them refuge in Gujarat, the King expressed concern over the assimilation of these foreigners in India. To address this concern, the four Dasturs, that is, elders, from the Parsee community, requested for a jar of milk and a spoon of sugar. One of the Dastur put the spoon of sugar in the milk to demonstrate that the Parsee community will become part of the local culture, like sugar dissolves in milk. Although they will retain their sweetness, that is, their distinct qualities and faith practices, they will adapt to local culture and add sweetness to it.

Like the Zoroastrians, many other communities travelled from far and wide, and found refuge in the Indian subcontinent. Our history is a testimony to many secular philosophies that enable us to cross the exclusionary boundaries of religious faith and to reinterpret our spiritual practice as encompassing all of humanity.

In Buddhist philosophy, for instance, right understanding or knowledge rests on individuals who recognize that composed reality is a partial picture of how things really are, that is, *yathabhutam*. Knowledge of the true nature of things as only partial and constructed is useful in developing appreciation and tolerance for the other partial truths about reality. This philosophical concept shares some strands of similarity with the theory of forms philosophized by Plato in a time and culture very distinct from the rise and spread of Buddhism in India. The theory of forms argues that our physical world, that is, the way we interpret our reality, is only a very imperfect imitation of absolute truth or form. Our truth, therefore, is constructed and reflects the limitations of our experiences, knowledge and understanding. These partial truths must be continually renewed with new meanings, based on the increase in our exposure to different perspectives of the world.

Many spiritual traditions in the Indian subcontinent, especially the traditions initiated by marginalized communities, emphasize the need to coexist and to practise peace and tolerance in our thoughts and actions. For instance, *Baul* are wandering village singers from Bengal who have no images, temples or ceremonials. In their songs, they criticize caste–class–religion based divisions in our societies. They propagate a syncretic religious sect that combines the lyrics from both the Hindu Bhakti movement and the Sufi traditions and seek to usher in humanism and empathy as the bedrocks of a tolerant and pluralistic society. Most of the Baul songs illustrate a beautiful synergy between Hindu and Muslim traditions and normalize the power of a tolerant society where people with differences can coexist.

In a Baul song, the singer chants, 'যে যা ভাবে সেই রুপে সে হয়, রাম-রহিমি-করিমি - কালী, এক আত্মা জগৎময়'[8] to emphasize that

---

[8] Translation: You may call the universal soul by the name and form that you find most enticing. The truth, however, is that Ram, Rahim, Karim or Kala are different names of the same supreme unifying force.

Ram, Rahim, Karim and Kala are the same as they all promote the idea of loving the other.

When one listens to Baul's music, one is listening to a spiritual tradition which is beyond any social boundaries—a space of freedom and an experience of deep love in the heart. Often the expression of 'being wounded' by a song is widely expressed by Baul masters; in many people's lives, it has happened that they unintentionally heard a Baul song, and it touched them so deeply that it changed everything. Baul songs invite everyone—it is an open space where all are welcome with or without their baggage. To be inclusive, you have to be accepting and tolerant. You have to have patience and embrace the differences. Our community worships differences because we know all these surface-level differences are tied with a common thread—the thread of humanity and love.

—Parvathy Baul, a Baul singer

Similar to the Baul singers are poets, artists and saints of the Bhakti movement in the Indian subcontinent who aimed to bridge the chasm between Hindus and Muslims, upper and lower castes or Dalits, between different regional cultures and sexes. The Bhakti movement promoted the religion of love, tolerance and compassion as a bedrock of an emancipated society. It was an anguished but peaceful protest against orthodox, casteist or classist societal traditions by promoting common participation, shared goals and making spiritual spaces and experiences accessible to everyone. The Bhakti movement was strengthened by the work of Sufi saints and peers who challenged Islamic orthodoxy and combined Vedantic philosophy and Buddhism in an attempt to question the Islamic doctrine of one truth and one God. Sufi saints such as Khwaja Moinuddin Chishti and Fariduddin Ganjshakar preached about love and tolerance and were highly revered across several faith communities. Their verses appealed to the universal emotions and morals of love and compassion, and were also referred to in Adi Granth, a Sikh religious text. This intertextuality, that is, adopting ideas from other religions, resonates with the practice of tolerance, wherein traditions are evaluated for their benefit to the common goal of humanity and all the principles, teachings or actions that further this goal are accepted unanimously. Although this practice of creating possibilities for differences to coexist by focusing on similarity and shared interests has antecedents in the past, it is devotedly followed in our present times. Many ethnographers are intrigued by the variety of rituals practised at dargahs that are a symbol of the synergy between Hindu and Muslim traditions. At Ajmer Sharif Dargah in Rajasthan or Haji Ali in Mumbai, it is observed that Hindus bend and touch their forehead to the ground in prayers. Many places, like a dargah, act as a site of congruence and convergence, where different religious communities bring their own practices and beliefs to enhance and enrich the texture and complexity of religious experience. Diverse rituals give rise to a multi-confessional community where different religions speak their truth in the service of a common shared goal. They all enter this place as disciples of the same God— each possessing only a partial truth.

When people cultivate tolerance towards others, they make conscious efforts to sympathize, if not empathize with others to understand why people are different and why they believe and behave in the ways they do. This process sensitizes us to other people's sufferings and pains.

In the Buddhist philosophy, tolerance is equated with the presence of an awakened heart, *bodhicitta*, a heart that feels the pain of others regardless of social, religious and class difference. Pema Chodron, a teacher in the Tibetan Buddhist tradition, defines tolerance as a practice to be proactive amid the growing state of conflict and hopelessness.[9] Tolerance is a strategy in actively sending out love in response to the constant negativity that one receives. The practice of *tonglen*, she explains, is to absorb the pain of this world in an in-breath, and to share with others all the love and compassion that we can gather in an out-breath. It emphasizes the need to go beyond our personal interests, motives and beliefs to feel compassion for others.

THE LOVE THAT WILL NOT DIE

(*When Things Fall Apart* by Pema Chodron)

The father of a two-year-old talks about turning on the television and unexpectedly seeing the bombing of the federal building in Oklahoma City. He watched as the firemen carried the limp and bloody bodies of the toddlers from the ruins of the day care centre on the building's first floor. He says that in the past he was able to distance himself from other people's suffering. But since he's become a father, things have changed. He feels as if each of those children was his child. He feels the grief of all the parents as his own grief.

This kinship with the suffering of others, this inability to continue to regard it from afar, is the discovery of our soft spot, the discovery of *bodhicitta*. *Bodhicitta* is a Sanskrit word that means 'noble or awakened heart'. It is said to be present in all beings. Just as butter is inherent in milk and oil is inherent in sesame seed, this soft spot is inherent in you and me.

---

[9] P. Chodron, *When Things Fall Apart: Heart Advice for Difficult Times* (Boulder, CO: Shambhala, 2016).

Like Buddhism, Jain traditions also stress that training in tolerance and non-violence is indispensable. According to the Jain philosophy, people study the world around them before they develop ways and methods to engage with it. Jainism suggests two cornerstones for engaging with others and the changes or differences that we witness in our societies: the logic of *nayavada* is the method of seven perspectives, and the logic of *syadvada* is the method of sevenfold assertions. The principle of *nayavada* negates the possibility of absolute truth and suggests that all the statements, opinions and beliefs we hold true have only a partial validity in the larger scheme of things. The second principle of *syadvada* suggests that assertions or judgements are conditional and that their validity depends on the context in which they occur. Jainism applies these two logics to the study of the relationship between the world and people and argues that any impression of the world and the people in it is, at best, only a single perspective or representation of reality (*ekanta*). Jainism encourages people to combine multiple perspectives, several partial truths and many valid representations (*anekanta*) while interacting with others and their surroundings. Although many scholars suggest that the virtues of acceptance and tolerance are projected inwards, that is, only towards the members of the Jain community, many contemporary Jain monks making efforts to reinterpret Jain philosophical traditions to address the needs of an increasingly globalized and plural world.

TOLERANCE HAS ITS CHALLENGES

Tolerance unsettles people as it compels them to let go of the certainty that they ascribe to their personal systems of belief and practice. We live in very fragile times, where things are changing rapidly. The birth of our nation is tied to the story of the bloodshed during the partition and continues to tarnish Hindu–Muslim relations. Our history is linked to several pain points inflicted by the British Raj and the spread of Christianity. The story of the natives of the

Indian subcontinent, the Dravidians, is replete with instances of Aryan violence and suppression. Caste- and gender-based violence have been part of our society for a long time. These collective memories of hatred and power struggles raise some questions: how do we move into a new world and leave this baggage behind? How do we practise tolerance and negotiate with differences in our lives every day? As a strategy to rethink our engagement with practices of tolerance in our interactions with others, we introduce the concept of *Sadharanikaran*—a communication model based on the Sanskrit concept of *Sahridaya*, that is, oneness to mitigate conflicts and tensions through tolerance and sensitivity.

EXPLORING THE INDIAN PHILOSOPHY OF *SAHRIDAYAS*

Sahridaya, or the oneness of the heart, is a state of existence that allows us to be attentive and to listen to others. The process of creating *Sahridaya* includes softening the space for people to feel welcomed and to participate. *Sahridaya* is inclusive; in this, it attempts to remove the fear of surveillance by inviting conversations among people with different voices and stories to share. *Sahridaya* is a conversational approach to bridge the gaps between different communities through which we can see each other more clearly and in a more positive light. *Sahridaya* is the attainment of commonality—the identification and pursuit of shared goals and interests—through the use of a language that is built with the intention of forging meaningful relations with others.

The Words We Use

We often use words casually without paying full attention to their implied meaning or the resulting effect on others. Reality is constituted through language—the words we use to describe our relationship with others. Words give us the power to connect with others or to build walls. With our words, we can either attain a state of oneness or make visible the existing crevices of hatred in our intercommunity relations.

The principle and practice of being a *Sahridaya* can be used to create spaces that can hold discomfort. *Sahridayas* are curious about blind spots in their thinking, and they are interested in stepping outside their prescribed social positions. They are willing to explore the alternative possibilities of being.

This state of acquiring equilibrium is only temporary, but the negotiations made during this phase can sediment into our routine practices. *Sahridayas* create a possibility of imagining a different present and future, a possibility in which we decide to shed our baggage of prejudice and hatred, our caste identities and class inequalities, the weight of the patriarchy on our societies and the hurt nestled in the past.

How can we enter a new world through this transition? We carry the stories of love, prejudice and discrimination in our bodies. We experience these emotions and situations through our bodies. In order to create the conditions of the *Sahridaya*, the body must be a witness to love, peace and tolerance. The body should be able to see, hear, feel and participate in practices rooted in the ethics of care and compassion.

The communication theory of the *Sahridaya* is interwoven with the concept of commonness, that is, the *sadharan*. Every day, it argues, is replete with possibilities for the body to experience love, enact care and extend support. Rebecca Solnit[10] suggests that, contrary to the common perception that humans are weak, selfish and divided, human nature is defined largely by virtues such as generosity and altruism that we practise on a daily basis. To bring out these virtues in our everyday lives, the theory of *Sahridaya* suggests that we pay attention to three things in our interactions

---

[10] Rebecca Solnit, *A Paradise Built in Hell: The Extraordinary Communities That Arise in Disaster* (New York, NY: Penguin Books, 2009).

with others, that is, what we are doing, why we are doing it and what would happen once we have done it. Actively thinking about outcomes may lead us to choose words that unite rather than divide us. This does not mean that we will have no differences. We will always have differences. Communication between the *Sahridayas* offer both a hope to dissolve the difference, if possible, and also an acceptance that some differences are unassimilable. Maybe we can create a new space altogether—a third, more cosmopolitan space, where differences do not capture all our attention as we look for new realities and identities. *Sahridaya* is, therefore, not a process of erasure but a process of making visible the vulnerability and risks in the task of assimilation and accommodation.

Like any new practice, it might be difficult in the beginning. It will never be a cakewalk, especially when people involved in the process are learning it at a different pace. It is a disorienting practice, because it entails removing the rug of certainty from underneath our feet as we step into new conversations. New conversations can help people forgive their past traumas and conflicts, thus encouraging them to imagine a better future despite seemingly irresolvable differences in our present. We must hold onto the last ounce of compassion and understanding in us as we create bridges and undo boundaries. We will encounter fear, threats, backlash and ridicule in our journey towards creating inclusive societies, but we can promise one thing. In the end, the struggle won't be for nothing.

Appiah explains this process very eloquently when he says[11]:

If someone really thinks that some group of people genuinely doesn't matter at all, he will suppose they are outside the circle of those to whom justifications are due. (That's why it is easier to think that animals don't matter than to think that people

---

[11] K. Appiah, *Cosmopolitanism: Ethics in a World of Strangers* (New York, NY: W. W. Norton & Company, 2007).

don't matter: animals can't ask us why we are abusing them.)
Still, if people really do think that some people don't
matter at all, there is only one thing to do: try to change
their minds, and, if you fail, make sure that they can't put
their ideas into action.

The real challenge to cosmopolitanism isn't the belief that
other people don't matter at all: it's the belief that they don't
matter very much. It's easy to get agreement that we have
some obligations to strangers. Perhaps, if their situation
becomes intolerable and we can do something about it at
a reasonable cost, we may even have a duty to intervene.
Perhaps we should stop genocide, intervene when there is
mass starvation or a great natural disaster. But must we do
more than this? I have been saying that we have obligations
to strangers. It is time, in closing, to say more about what
those obligations are.

—Kwame Anthony Appiah in *Cosmopolitanism:*
Ethics in a World of Strangers

CHAPTER 4

Opening Our
Hearts and Minds

Opening our hearts and minds to ideas and people that are unfamiliar and push us out of our echo chamber is like riding a roller coaster. It is refreshing and confusing, exciting and scary. Also, when we bring along our family and precious children on this ride, we are bound to feel responsible for their safety and well-being as much as we are thrilled by the rewards.

Examples of this process could include something as simple as the husband entering an unfamiliar terrain of helping his wife in household chores and taking equal responsibility for emotional labour in the family to something as complicated as expanding and enriching our social circles to meet people who are from different social backgrounds. For instance, it can be very difficult for a man to imagine himself cooking or changing diapers when all his life he has been socialized within a strict definition of what is masculine. Similarly, individuals who have been raised to uphold strict caste boundaries would find it challenging to introduce changes in their families by inviting people from a different caste, especially the low caste, to their homes.

Also, we must acknowledge that such changes can have consequences. For instance, if an upper-caste family decides to befriend people from the lower caste and invites them to family gatherings and celebrations such as wedding ceremonies and birthdays, they might face resistance from some of the other upper-caste guests. This can jeopardize their social relations and may compel them to retrace their steps. The question then is twofold: How can adults identify the social biases inherent in their thinking and practice? How can adults redesign their social environments, specifically their homes, to be as bias-free as possible?

We have developed a pragmatic four-step approach that is doable and tested. It draws from scholarly research and theory and, at the same time, can be successfully applied at home. We focus on two critical features of bias: *socialization* and *practice*. In other words, we design an approach that will help address two core questions: How do stereotypes and bias emerge and how can they be challenged, how are these prejudices practised (medium and content) and how can we enact tolerance? The four steps that guide us through this process are as follows:

1. Re-examining the process of socialization
2. Understanding privilege
3. Embracing the power of 'why' question
4. Challenging a single story

STEP I. RE-EXAMINING THE PROCESS OF SOCIALIZATION

We discussed in Chapter 1 that socialization is a process through which young people are inducted into the norms, values, beliefs and practices of their communities. It involves five steps. Let us understand each of these steps with an example of religious socialization. First, children are encouraged to identify with religious rituals and beliefs right from a young age. For instance, during their religious education classes for young children, many monotheistic religions emphasize that there is only 'one' true God and that people who believe in a different God are followers of Satan. As an inference, followers of polytheistic religions are labelled as offenders, and this may create a bias towards people from other religions. Second, children are fed with religious stories and narratives that promote and strengthen religious beliefs. Such narratives are not always intended to discriminate against other religions, but they always show one's own religion as superior and may be interpreted by parents and family members in ways that create among children a dislike towards religious differences. For instance, according to the traditions of Jain philosophy, humans should never harm other living beings. As a result, Jains are strictly vegetarian, and so are many Hindus. Problems arise when elders from the community encourage their children to stigmatize those who follow a meat-based diet. Well, vegetarianism has its virtues and, if the family believes in them, they must have the right to practise and also propagate this philosophy. However, foreboding all contact and interactions with non-vegetarians or refusing to sit at the same table with their other classmates because the others do not share their belief in a vegetarian lifestyle are extreme steps. Third, children are invited to participate in several community activities and rituals to strengthen their belief in the shared ideology of discrimination. For instance, several parents enrol their children in far-right religious organizations such as conservative Catholic schools, rigid Hindu organizations and orthodox madrasas, where they are involved in learning modules and games designed to cultivate a sense of hatred for anything that is not Christian, Hindu or Muslim enough.

In all these instances, as soon as children are born, they get a label of a religion and, thereafter, consistent efforts are made to educate them in accordance with the dominant religious guidelines. The process of socialization does not always occur actively, and people often don't realize that they are either socializing others or being socialized as members of a religious community. Identifying bias requires revisiting all the practices and experiences through which young people are initiated into a religious ideology. Shall we do a quick exercise?

Let us start by studying our routines. What are some of the everyday mandatory religious activities for your family members at home? Pay close attention to such religious routines and communications that take place around them.

Kiran conducted a study with Hindu and Muslim parents of students in the schools of Bangalore, Ahmedabad and Delhi, and her many conversations with them revealed some ways in which bias and hatred towards the religious other is communicated in and through everyday conversations and spaces. For instance, many young boys who offer *namaaz* at mosques have sometimes initiated or participated in discussions related to the divine superiority of the Islamic community over other religions, the political theory of radical Islam that suggests that Muslims will be able to establish a worldwide caliphate in the future, and some comments bashing Hindus as lesser humans. Similarly, many Hindu parents share WhatsApp messages with their children bashing the Muslim community as violent, outsiders and conservatives. In neither case do elders from the family or the teachers invest time in addressing these biases. These everyday biases are also practised as humour— though children and parents claim that humour is harmless, it teaches young people that making fun of and insulting members of a different religious community is acceptable. Careful study of our everyday conversations is the first step towards identifying how, as adults, we instil feelings of animosity and prejudice in the minds of our children.

We can also examine our socialization to see where and how we routinely pick up gender stereotypes. Let us take the example of a derogatory term commonly used in high schools for girls, that is, 'slut'. Historically, the term had negative connotations and was used to refer to a woman with low standards of cleanliness. With time, this term is used as a flippant insult for women who own and act out their sexual desires. It is often used as an abuse to shame young girls because 'women's sexuality' continues to be a taboo topic in India. Young girls are slut-shamed and bullied, whereas boys who are sexually active are labelled 'studs' and 'players'.

This patriarchal tendency to slut-shame young girls for their sexual choices has spiralled into a more complex debate around sexual violence and rape. Young girls and women who are survivors of sexual assaults and violence are often slut-shamed, and this prevents them from reporting the crime. Our patriarchal society pins down concepts of dignity to the vagina of a woman, and any girl who is sexually violated is considered to be dirty or less dignified. Although there is growing awareness around this, even today, when families are trying to arrange a marriage alliance for their son, they demand that the would-be bride be a virgin. This is never a consideration for the groom.

Let us look at some of the personality traits and how, because of our socialization, we perceive them differently in the case of men and women.

Trait	Boys/Men	Girls/ Women
Assertive	A boy who is assertive is called a leader.	A girl who is assertive is called bossy.
Sensitive	A boy who is sensitive is called a 'pussy' (weak).	A girl who is sensitive is called kind and generous.
Extrovert	A boy who is an extrovert is called social.	A girl who is an extrovert is called lose, gossipmonger or morally weak.
Career-oriented	A boy who is career-oriented is called focused.	A woman who is career-oriented is called a home-breaker and blamed for not prioritizing her family.
Firm	A boy who is firm is called determined.	A girl who is firm is called dominating and inconsiderate.
Family oriented	A man who wants to spend time with his family is called *joru ka gulam* or a 'sissy'.	A woman who wants to spend time with her family is called dutiful.

Children use stories, movies, games and other forms of popular culture to structure their imagination, to limit the scope of what they can do and who they can be. When we complete the first step of re-examining our socialization, we broaden the imaginative scope for young boys and girls. We will discuss this aspect in detail in Chapter 6.

STEP II. UNDERSTANDING PRIVILEGE

What is privilege? In simple words, privilege is a special right, advantage or immunity granted or available only to a particular person or group. You must have heard terms such as white privilege, male privilege and rich privilege. Of course, hard work, the position that we have earned or self-made wealth can also bring us certain privileges, but much of the privilege is acquired by the mere virtue of the conditions we are born in—your caste, gender, family name and wealth or just your skin colour!

Interestingly, privilege is often invisible to those who have it. People who claim that they do not see caste and that our urban societies no longer practise caste-based segregation and discrimination generally belong to the upper-caste and/or class communities. They are probably shielded from the violence of the caste system and poverty, and hence oblivious to it. The choice to be neutral towards the caste system or to refuse to identify existing forms of caste hierarchies is a privilege in action.

Checking our privilege is an important step in recognizing how the system might be benefiting us and harming others, or vice versa.

'Privilege' in action includes the following:

1. Ignoring uncomfortable social realities because you are not affected by them.
2. Ignoring instances of violence that others face because you do not belong to a marginalized or oppressed community.

3. Criticizing marginalized communities for demanding their rights by disqualifying their experiences as invalid; also blaming the victim.
4. Assuming authority over people's experiences and speaking for them.

Let us use the following checklist to identify our own privilege or lack of it.

Check your privilege

Primary education ☐

Secondary education ☐

Family house ☐

Regular family income ☐

Unrestricted access to
public places (temples/
community garden-spaces)
and people's houses ☐

Unrestricted access to services ☐
(electricity, the Internet,
water, cooking gas)

Brahmin/Kshatriya/Vaishya/ ☐
other higher caste

If you checked most of the boxes, you have a lot of privileges that other people from a low-caste/class community or a different gender may not enjoy. These privileges give you or your family a vantage point not accessible to everyone. For instance, if your child needs extra coaching and help for their studies and you are able to afford it, the child would have had a better start and a higher chance of getting into a merit list. On the contrary, your child's classmates who may have enrolled in the school under the Right to Education Act may not be able to pay for extra coaching and guidance, may be spending many hours helping their parents in chores or investing time on a job to support the family. Additionally, students who belong to low-caste communities may also have to deal with the everyday insult, abuse and mockery due to their caste identity. Poor children lack quiet spaces to study and do not have access to even the basic educational facilities, such as books or the Internet. Young people who have so many things to deal with every day while also fight for their survival will find it difficult to concentrate on studies the way privileged children do.

We had once conducted a semi-structured interview with two of our colleagues—one man and one woman—who were at beginner level administrative roles. We just asked them to describe their mornings before leaving for office. This is what the newly married woman said:

> Wake up at 5:30, make tea for self and mother-in-law, start making breakfast and food for tiffin boxes, when husband and father-in-law wake up, make tea for them, serve breakfast, get husband's stuff for office ready, get all the tiffin boxes to carry to work ready, get ready for office, catch the bus.

This is what the newly married man said, 'Wake up at eight, have tea, read the newspaper, take a shower when things are ready in the bathroom, eat breakfast, collect the tiffin box and leave for office on my scooter.'

Step II of the process leads to an understanding of the privilege that we and others enjoy. It also helps you to open your hearts in empathy to those less privileged. As we proceed to Step III, we start by asking how did we get here? Why are certain groups privileged just because of a label they got at birth?

STEP III. EMBRACING THE POWER OF 'WHY' QUESTIONS

Let's begin with some introspection.

When your child asks you a difficult question, how often do you say...

1. Children do not need to know this
   □ Always □ Sometimes □ Never

2. You should not be questioning your elders
   □ Always □ Sometimes □ Never

3. This disrespect is the result of watching angrezi shows on your phones
   □ Always □ Sometimes □ Never

4. When we were young, we used to simply follow what our elders told us; no questions asked
   □ Always □ Sometimes □ Never

5. This is an inappropriate question
   □ Always □ Sometimes □ Never

6. You can challenge my decision when you earn your own money and live in your own house
   □ Always □ Sometimes □ Never

7. My house, my rules
   □ Always □ Sometimes □ Never

8. You have this audacity because we have given you so much freedom
   ☐ Always ☐ Sometimes ☐ Never
9. Go to your room—right now
   ☐ Always ☐ Sometimes ☐ Never

As parents and teachers, we often get irritated with the 'why' questions our children ask us. When we are at the limit of our patience, we also have a favourite response, 'because I say so'. If we intend to raise our children as problem-solvers and innovative thinkers, we must encourage them to ask 'why' questions. Trying to investigate the 'why' for what we advise, believe in and practise is important for instilling critical and logical thinking skills in our children and in ourselves. Addressing the 'why' for everything children are requested to accomplish and do is useful for three main reasons:

1. When children know why doing something is important, they feel more involved and motivated.
2. When children know the reasons for believing in and practising something, they can either support these practices or challenge them in meaningful ways. This ensures that our age-old traditions are constantly reinterpreted and modified to make them more relevant to changing times.
3. Why questions compel children and parents to think more analytically.

Interestingly, many religious, caste-based and gender-related texts from where we borrow stories, teachings and examples are regressive and old. These texts were composed years ago in response to the realities prevalent in the societies of the past. Understanding the context in which these texts were created helps us challenge notions that their advice is timeless. Evaluating the context requires us to give up our argument that these books are 'true or false' and engage in more nuanced conversations on how changing times require for us to reinterpret their lessons.

PAUSE AND THINK

What are some ancient sayings about women, Dalits and religions that make no sense now?

Let us also spend some time answering these difficult questions:

1. Why do we say things like, 'He is from a lower caste, but you wouldn't believe it if you visit his home! He looks and lives just like us...'
2. Why do we let children believe that those who aren't doing well in life are lazy?
3. Why do we believe that the wife's parents should not expect anything from the couple, but that the husband's parents have all the rights over their time, money and also the right to dictate their life choices?
4. Why do we believe that it is the man's responsibility to fulfil all the material desires of his family members?
5. Why do we believe that when women marry and have children, they naturally cannot/shouldn't have career ambitions?
6. Why don't we think of Dalit deaths in police custody in India when we protest George Floyd's murder and police brutality in the USA?
7. Why do we limit the focus of our conversations about women in positions of leadership to their saris, appearance, relations and kids?

8. Why do we automatically assume that our daughter will be happier if she marries an engineer rather than a school teacher?
9. Why do we think that equality means bringing women 'up' to the male standard? Why are jobs and professions that have been associated with work that women do often ill-paid and less respected?
10. As soon as we hear of a mass shooting or terrorist attack anywhere in the world, why do we assume that the accused is a Muslim?

Facing Discomfort with Comfort

Children are naturally inquisitive and curious. They want to participate in adult-led discussions at dinner tables and family gatherings. All we have to do as parents is nurture that curiosity. The question then is: how do we deal with the discomfort that we feel when our children question our authority? How do we get ready to face discomfort and share power with our children?

As parents, the first step towards initiating a relationship on the basis of transparency and shared authority with our children is to see them as independent thinkers who can speak for themselves. We should take a step back from representing them, speaking on their behalf and assuming that 'we know what is best for them'. An easy way to get started is to become 'better listeners' and ask more questions. Ask your children how they feel, what they think and what they believe. Ask them if they would want things to be different at home, and ask them for suggestions on how to make those changes.

While addressing questions raised by children, we should spend some time researching issues, beliefs and values if we do not know enough. It is perfectly fine to say, 'I don't know, or I haven't given this enough thought. Let us find out more.' A starting point here is to acknowledge that 'parents may not know everything.' Accepting that we are still learning to be better parents and citizens helps us to identify possible progressive values and to implement new practices in our own families if we find merit in them.

Let us look at a parent's testimony on how they changed the way they address their domestic help when their children expressed that they were uncomfortable with the term *kamwali bai*.

SUJATA IS FAMILY...

I had to resume working immediately after my pregnancy; I was offered a three-month maternity leave. We interviewed a lot of domestic helps for childcare purposes and finally hired Sujata. She has been taking care of my son Rahul ever since. Rahul is very attached to her and calls her *tai*. We call Sujata by her name when she is around, but once she leaves, we would unknowingly start using the word *kamwali* while talking about her in the family. As Rahul started understanding and mastering language, he would constantly repeat the word *tai* every time we used the word *kamwali* in our family. For a long time, we saw this as Rahul's way of telling us that he has started making associations and recognizing people. It was only later when he could speak small sentences that he expressed he did not like it when the parents addressed as *kamwali*. Now, Rahul is very young, and he doesn't really understand the literal meaning of the word, but he sure felt something that made him sense that we were unintentionally distancing her from our family, like she wasn't family. Rahul used to say, 'Stop Mumma, no *kamwali*, only *tai*', every time we used the word *kamwali*. When we realized how hurt he felt, we started using our help's name even in her absence. This incident, however, made me realize two things. First, language is powerful and can be used to practise class, gender and so much more and, second, our children can make us more sensitive towards others.

STEP IV. CHALLENGING A SINGLE STORY

Chimamanda Adichie is a Nigerian writer who gave a thought-provoking TED talk about the dangers of a single story. She explains how her imagination of 'what kind of characters could exist in literature' drew inspiration from American British stories set in foreign Western lands. These characters had no resemblance with Adichie's life in Nigeria. Creating narratives about communities from a distance, using a single lens, and portraying them as problematic or inferior, has a strong negative impact.

EXCERPT FROM THE TED TALK: THE DANGER OF A SINGLE STORY

It is impossible to talk about the single story without talking about power. There is a word, an Igbo word, that I think about whenever I think about the power structures of the world, and it is *nkali*. It's a noun that loosely translates to 'to be greater than another'. Like our economic and political worlds, stories too are defined by the principle of *nkali*. How they are told, who tells them, when they're told, how many stories are told are really dependent on power.

Power is the ability not just to tell the story of another person, but to make it the definitive story of that person. The Palestinian poet Mourid Barghouti writes that if you want to dispossess people, the simplest way to do it is to tell their story and to start with, 'secondly'. Start the story with the arrows of the Native Americans, and not with the arrival of the British, and you have an entirely different story. Start the story with the failure of the African state, and not with the colonial creation of the African state, and you have an entirely different story....

The single story creates stereotypes. And the problem with stereotypes is not that they are untrue, but that they are incomplete. They make one story become the only story. I've always felt that it is impossible to engage properly with a place or a person without engaging with all of the stories of that place and that person. The consequence of the single story is this: it robs people of dignity. It makes our recognition of our equal humanity difficult. It emphasizes how we are different rather than how we are similar.

—Chimamanda Adichie

THEORY SPEAK/SCHOLAR SPEAK

Stuart Hall is a well-known communication scholar who taught us that any piece of communication—a film, a song, a story or even a picture—can be approached in three different ways.

The first approach is called dominant reading. It is a hegemonic approach in which you accept what the author intends to convey without apprehension and at face-value. The second approach is called negotiated reading in which you accept some parts of the arguments. The third approach is called oppositional reading in which you critically look at what is being said and provide an interpretation that challenges the popular, dominant or widely accepted interpretation.

Let us understand this with an example. Are you familiar with the story of Eklavya and Dronacharya from Mahabharata? In a nutshell, when Dronacharya refused to accept Eklavya as his student on the grounds that he trained only upper-caste boys, Eklavya decided to self-train himself in archery on the basis of what Eklavya could secretly gather from observing Drona teaching his students. When Dronacharya realized that Eklavya had mastered the art of archery and was a tough competition for his students, he requested Eklavya to cut off his thumb and offer it to Dronacharya as *guru dakshina*.

Now, we remember studying this story in school. The ultimate lesson we drew from the story was what a great and self-sacrificing student Eklavya was. That is how a student should be. Did you read this story? Were you ever encouraged to question Drona's action of asking for Eklavya's thumb? Did we ever see this as a story of a higher-caste person's unjust domination of a lower-caste person? If we did, that is oppositional reading, and this is what we need to do with many of our well-accepted stories—from every religion, mythology and culture.

Such oppositional reading can also be practised on some of the popular ads that we see. In fact, spotting bias in ads and creating alternative ads has been a very helpful way to encourage critical thinking.

Similar exercise can be done with media stories we encounter every day. Rather than denying that such discriminatory systems exist, or claiming that 'we don't believe in such discrimination as we don't look at anybody's caste or religion' acknowledge the persistent bias in the system. Use newspaper articles to initiate discussions around the caste system in India and narrate stories of people who worked hard to abolish this discriminatory practice. For instance, *The Boy Who Asked Why: The Story of Bhimrao Ambedkar* is a very inspiring children's book summarizing Ambedkar's lifetime of fight for equality. Another interesting book for young people in the age group of 14–16 years can be *Breast Stories* by Mahasweta Devi. It is an anthology of three short fiction stories highlighting the plight of lower-caste women and their efforts to subvert the patriarchy. These stories demonstrate how two or more marginalized identities intersect (here, women and low caste) and lead to serious discrimination. Similarly, parents and adults can discuss the life and philosophy of Mahatma Gandhi, who actively worked, collaborated with and encouraged lower-caste communities. For youth in their late teens, it would also be interesting to discuss the criticism of Gandhi's approach to supporting low-caste communities. This could also be a good opportunity to discuss racism in North America and Europe, where African Americans and indigenous people have faced persistent abuse.

Adults can introduce children to stories, games and media that help them imagine an alternative world and challenge heteronormativity and gender binaries. Why not start with a retelling of the famous fairy tales like Cinderella, Snow White and Mermaid so that characters are not relegated to definite gender roles? Why not gift your children feminist books and read with them? Every young person should have access to feminist ideas, texts and experiences because patriarchy oppresses people from all gender orientations, not just women. Here is an international list of books that help us think more deeply about gender.

Feminist Books for Your Woke Child

Title of the Book	Author	Publisher	Age Range
Satrangi Boys	Kamla Bhasin	Pratham Books	3–6 years
Satrangi Girls	Kamla Bhasin	Pratham Books	3–6 years
It's Okay to be Different	Todd Parr	Little, Brown Books for Young Readers	3–6 years
Mary Wears What She Wants	Keith Negley	HarperCollins	4–8 years
Teddy's Favorite Toy	Christian Trimmer and Madeline Valentine	Atheneum Books for Young Readers	4–8 years

Title of the Book	Author	Publisher	Age Range
Dear Boy	Paris Rosenthal, Jason Rosenthal and Holly Hatam	HarperCollins	4–8 years
A Wrinkle in Time	Madeleine L'Engle	Square Fish	6–14 years
Malala: My Story of Standing Up for Girls' Rights	Malala Yousafzai	Little, Brown Books for Young Readers	7–10 years
The Restless Girls	Jessica Burton	Bloomsbury Children's Books	8–10 years
Good Night Stories for Rebel Girls	Francesca Cavallo and Elena Favilli	Timbuktu Labs	10–13 years
Here We Are: Feminism for the Real World	Kelly Jensen	Algonquin Young Readers	12–16 years
We Should All be Feminists	Chimamanda Ngozi Adichie	Anchor Books	13 years and above

The most effective way of helping young people develop a comprehensive understanding of any social system is to show them how the history and present of the system interact—where and how the system originated, how it de-evolved and the ways in which it manifests in the present.

THE CONUNDRUM OF RESERVATION POLICY

Is reservation unjust, a reverse casteism or a way to ensure equal representation? We know many people who have lost an admission or job because of the reservation policy. They complain bitterly about the injustice of it. We feel their pain, of course. But why do we forget that for hundreds of years such injustice has been done to those whose gain people now resent and why?

At the end of the chapter, we would like to share a few thoughts on reinventing parenting and embracing a parenting style that would help our children to open their hearts and minds to new ideas and people. We begin with some myths that we love as parents and how they do more harm than help our children.

Parenting Myths

Our parenting and education practices are influenced by many myths. Here we discuss a few.

Myth 1: Our children must be ahead in the race by any means. Fixed standardized curriculum, textbooks and schools with posh infrastructures are what our children need to be ahead in the race.

If by race we mean the rat race, remember that even if we win the rat race, we are still rats! Textbook-based education systems fail to provide real-life experiences to children. In a constantly changing and dynamic society, in a world that is ever more connected through media and technology, our children must learn to be curious, resilient and adaptable. When we consider 21st-century skills, the qualities that come first to mind include teamwork, leadership, agility, capacity for innovation and emotional intelligence. This can only be achieved through experiential learning.

Myth 2: Children are too immature to be exposed to social and political issues, and giving them access to material outside of curriculum will distract them from their studies.

To raise curious minds, we must introduce children to real-world issues, including those related to politics, the environment, social practices, culture, religion, violence and inequalities, right from a young age. Of course, this must be done gradually and in an age-appropriate manner.

Many parents feel that they should cocoon their children and keep them away from complex issues related to politics, culture, religion and gender. Sometimes, parents who can afford to keep their children sheltered from the societal problems affecting millions in our country are in positions of privilege and so they are unaffected by these issues and the resulting inequalities. On other occasions, parents think that children should just focus on their education and not be bothered by what is happening in the society. As a result, when children ask us questions about political and social issues or when they question religious and cultural practices at home, parents tend to scold them into submission by saying, 'You are a child, you must simply follow the instructions' or 'children do not ask such questions' or 'this is not your place to speak.'

Addressing children's questions can be a wonderful way to initiate conversations around gender, religion, caste and class. Adults must create a learning environment where children feel safe to ask any question that comes to their mind, challenge common practices and customs or at least express their discomfort about certain practices.

Families can be harnessed as fertile sites to discuss issues related to class, gender, religion, caste and to practise 'difference'. Some ways in which parents can use family gatherings and common places to introduce children to such issues include the following:

1. Reading, watching and listening to news together and discussing how each member feels about the way events and people and events are portrayed and discussed.

2. Paying close attention to commercials and using these as texts to unpack issues such as gender discrimination, body shaming, the invisibility of certain groups of people, promoting commercial interests at the cost of health and well-being of people and others.

3. Practising change in our homes by adopting new and progressive family norms and traditions. More gender-balanced practices, especially related to division of labour, encouraging children to befriend students from different sociocultural and economic backgrounds and discussing sensitive topics related to caste and religion at dinner tables.

4. Find meaningful media, such as films, documentaries, podcasts and YouTube videos, to watch together with children. Believe us, there are so many good movies out there, and many times our children are the best source for recommending them.

Myth 3: Children, especially boys, participating in household chores is beneath our social status and would take time away from studies.

Making children responsible for certain home chores is a proven practice to teaching them basic life skills. When children participate in household work, they learn to be responsible, accomplish tasks, appreciate work and develop good work ethics. This also ensures that the family becomes more gender equal. Once they experience how much efforts go into tasks such as cooking, cleaning, grocery shopping and small repairs, they are kind to household help and other workers. Rotating home chores between sons and daughters as well as parents also helps them to appreciate what they have taken for granted.

Myth 4: People's worth is judged by the brands they use and the luxury goods they possess, so it is our duty as parents to provide our children with all the comforts, luxuries and branded items they demand. Their friends will value them accordingly.

Quite the contrary. First, if our children learn to judge people on the basis of their possessions, they are likely to miss out on some great friendships and experiences. Also, they will not learn to appreciate the hard work that goes into producing wealth. Entitled children become entitled adults and fail to appreciate the rights and preferences of other people.

Moving further from the family set-up, we should also see how our parenting affects the larger society. Education can be a social movement built on the practice of listening to differences, acknowledging diverse perspectives and nurturing pluralism in our society. For instance, many social science textbooks in India introduce concepts related to our Indian constitution, fundamental rights and duties, and other civic issues. Children learn that, according to our Indian constitution, no person can be discriminated against on the basis of their gender, caste, religion and class. This learning, however, doesn't reflect the true state of affairs in many parts of the country, as we have seen in previous chapters. The question then is: how can we broaden our textbook-based education to address the social issues of our times? How can we use homes and classrooms as educational spaces to teach our young to uphold their moral obligations towards the principles of equality and justice? How can we use critical learning to enable our children to be responsible citizens?

Reinvent Parenting
From Obedience to Engagement

Would you like if your children do everything you want them to? They obediently follow all of your instructions, are exceptional in studies, high achievers in sports and all hobbies and do all the household chores with a smile. They respect the choice you make for them. They never argue, never question and never criticize you. Heaven, right? Well, such a home is the worst place for a child to grow up and become a responsible and independent adult. Also, there is a high chance that the child's own happiness and self-esteem would be highly compromised.

Situation I

Shyam is a teenage boy who is very scared of his parents. His parents are extremely strict and expect their son to follow their instructions. One of their rules includes prohibiting Shyam from attending house parties with his friends. They are afraid that Shyam may fall prey to bad company, begin to consume substances and become friends with girls. All valid fears, but Shyam is so terrified of them that he never discusses anything about school and friends at home.

He has recently started experiencing attraction towards his classmate and wants to befriend her. He also wants to attend house parties, so he decides to sneak out at night without telling his parents. He comes home before the daybreak, and his parents know nothing about it.

He is doing everything he wants to do without his parents' approval. The constant sneaking out and staying up till late is influencing his schoolwork and grades.

His parents think he is very obedient and focused. They do not know the reason for his poor academic performance. They are worried, but have no idea what is causing him to lose interest in schoolwork.

One night, as Shyam sneaks out again, he rides on a motorbike with his friend and meets with an accident. Shyam is so terrified of his parents that he decides not to tell them anything. His parents find out only when they get a call from the hospital. They are very upset with Shyam as they feel they have been betrayed.

Situation II

Rahil is a teenage boy who tops his class. He has straight As and is often awarded 'best student of the year' awards and certificates. He shares a very open and easy relationship with his parents.

His parents never punish Rahil. They ask him to reflect and think through his actions and to make up for his mistakes in some meaningful ways. Instead of calling a 'timeout' or 'grounding' him, they encourage him to participate in healthy activities to make up for his bad behaviour. As remedials for his mistakes, he is sometimes required to spend time cleaning his room/house, writing an essay on what he did and if he thinks it is wrong, or helping his parents in their work. There are times when Rahil doesn't agree that his actions were wrong or unethical. In such situations, his parents listen to his arguments and re-evaluate their interpretation. For instance, the school once sent a complaint to his parents that Rahil was bullying some students in his class. When his parents approached and reprimanded him, he explained that he was taking a stand for himself. He was, in fact, standing up against the bullies in his class who would mock and degrade him by calling him names such as 'sissy', 'pussy' and 'nerd disaster'. When he threatened to fight them if they continued to bully, they backed off but later complained to their teacher that Rahil was bullying them. When the parents heard his side of the story, they believed Rahil and apologized for assuming that it was his fault. They even encouraged him to go see the teacher and explain his point.

Rahil has learned to evaluate the outcomes of intended actions and is quick to accept responsibility when things go wrong. Even when he makes a huge mistake, he isn't afraid to own it up because he knows his parents will help him make amends and better the situation.

What do we learn from these two situations? Situation I is an example of strict parenting where adults treat children as 'unthinking', 'immature' and 'dependent' individuals who need to be compelled to do the right thing. In this kind of parenting, adults 'dictate terms' to their children, and there's very little room for discussion, dialogue or exchange. This style follows a top-down approach, and children find it difficult to express their grievances, doubts or disappointments with their parents.

Strict or Authoritarian Parenting

At the root of their strictness is a deep-seated fear of the future and safety of their children, but strict parenting deprives children of the opportunity to evaluate their actions—to understand how they affect them and the people around them. When children continuously receive instructions from their parents on what to do, they find it difficult to develop their own sense of discretion about right and wrong, good and bad. Strict parenting does not nourish the child; it scares them into submission and cultivates in them a lifelong habit to bow to power. Children's first encounter with power may manifest in instances where it is used to threaten and bully others. Also, such children find it more difficult to develop the use of critical thinking when confronted with the orders from someone in power.

There is also another factor that prompts strict parenting—looking at our children as an instrument to enhance our social prestige and image. Our personal aspirations prevent us from recognizing children as independent people who have their own desires and temperaments.

Power grants us privileges and can be used to either build others or break them. When parents use their power and authority to compel their children into submission, they indicate that

1. Power translates into no accountability. No one can question our decisions, ask for a justification or give a rationale. Powerful people can 'force' less powerful people to 'obey' their orders.
2. Acquiring a position of power and authority means exercising dominance over others. This includes threatening others, punishing them and treating them as inferiors; it is seldom used to help others grow and thrive.
3. Having power means that all of our decisions are meant to be correct. Power protects us from accepting our mistakes, apologizing or changing our behaviour.

Children should learn to associate power with a sense of responsibility and an accountability of one's actions. Fear of adults and harsh punishments may compel children to control their behaviour to please their parents, but such measures of discipline do not give children the opportunity to understand when and how their demands or conduct become unethical or wrong.

For children to be independent thinkers and leaders, parents must develop a parenting style wherein they treat their children as equals and independent thinking individuals. Such a parenting style recognizes that children have the right to make choices and decisions about their lives. That, of course, does not mean that there are no family guidelines about what is acceptable and what is not. In our research with youth, they have time and again told us that they value adult guidance and support in their lives when it is done in the right manner. Involving children in creating these guidelines is the first step in a more thoughtful parenting style.

Involved Parenting

In the involved parenting style, we try to validate our children's emotions, listen to them and establish shared ground rules; instead of punishing, we encourage children to make amends and dish out responsibility with freedom. Children raised in this manner learn the value of self-discipline and abide by the rules made through deliberation and discussion. It fosters a relationship of equals between parents and children in such a way that children are motivated to practise good behaviour out of care and respect instead of fear.

Let us look at some strategies that can be used to raise children as active participants at homes, schools and in societies.

1. Encourage responsive interactions where children's ideas, thoughts and opinions are openly received and valued. Children should have a place at the decision-making table with parents and other members of the family. At school, this can be observed in the freedom that a student enjoys in contributing to their lesson plans and learning outcomes.

   Ask children questions that will make them think about and express their feelings. Asking the following questions is an interesting way to initiate children into the decision-making process: What do you think? What do you want? What will you choose? How can we do it differently?

2. Encourage children to establish their own routines with your guidance. Make sure these routines help them evolve into better thinkers, innovators and empaths.

3. Acknowledge children's contribution and opinions at home by highlighting how their participation helped with decision-making.

4. Encourage children to take the lead in their life's events. Support them from a distance but allow them to make mistakes. Encourage them to choose ways to make amendments for those mistakes or unacceptable behaviour. Ideal ways to make amendments involve doing something that would help them reflect on their behaviour and identify ways to either alter it or avoid repeating it in the future. Writing an essay or an apology, for instance, can help them reflect on why and how their actions hurt them or others.

5. Invite children to provide feedback on our parenting style and take those suggestions into consideration. For instance, if children feel that a certain rule in the family's shared guidelines needs to be changed, genuinely consider changing the guideline or including an exception that makes the said guideline less severe in nature.

We know that this is not always easy to accept when our conventional wisdom has repeatedly told us about the virtues of punishment. We worry that such freedom will make our children disrespectful, and we will lose control over them. That is precisely the problem with conventional wisdom, because respect cannot be earned by fear or force, and even when control can offer some short-term advantages, in the long-term, dialogue wins over control. We enlist some recommendations that parents can use to develop their own style of involved parenting.

1. Apologizing when we misuse our power and hurt younger members of the family.
2. Respect young adults' choices if they decide to adopt or experiment with a practice that is not a family tradition; for example, not participating in certain religious rituals, choosing vegetarianism or deciding to consume meat, following sustainable fashion where they don't want to buy unnecessary clothes or clothes from certain brands that are abusing labour. We might not like some of these choices for sure, and we have all the right to present our arguments in favour of our choice. If children are very young, we may tell them that they can make this choice only after they are 18 or whatever age seems reasonable, but ultimately we will have to allow young adults to make their life choices.
3. Refrain from the 'I told you so' response. Many times, children make a bad choice, realize their mistake and want to confess it. As parents, we must make it easy for them to admit their mistakes instead of shaming them.

We understand that this is going to be the toughest part. We cherish our values and our beliefs, and we often assume that they are ideal and noble. We also have good reasons why we have chosen them. We may also not agree with everything our children want and say, and we don't have to. Again, involving children in meaning-making and decision-making processes does not mean that parents shouldn't continue providing guidance and even disciplining their children. The focus, we believe, should be on ensuring that power is negotiated and children have the rights to question the norms. We should also make deliberate efforts to address their concerns about authority and how it is exercised in families.

CHAPTER 5

Unlearning Together

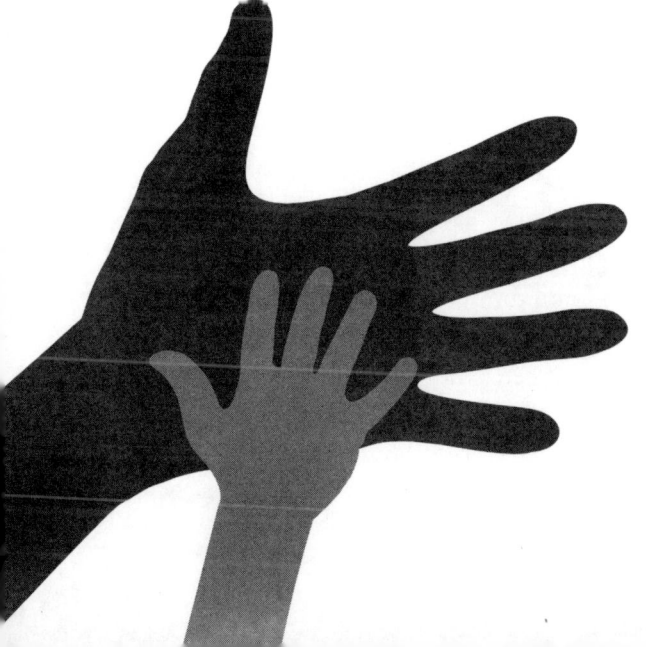

Unlearning is the most difficult kind of learning. Unlearning involves re-examining our daily habits, beliefs and practices, our inherited and acquired baggage. Why is it important to unlearn together and to learn together? Research on social and behavioural change shows that it is very difficult for individuals to accept and practise new behaviours if their communities do not adopt change. The community includes extended family members, neighbours, family friends and neighbourhood organizations. Our extended community circles play a very strong role in keeping us limited to our caste, class, gender and religious roles, and the pressure they create can prevent us from expanding our horizons. The definition of community is fluid because we can have different communities on the basis of our needs and identities. For instance, a Hindu family can be a member of the ISKCON community on the basis of their religious beliefs and identities, and the same family may belong to an elite club depending on their economic status and position in the society. On the other hand, a Dalit family may strongly identify with Dalit congregations and families in their neighbourhood as they question the Hindu caste system in India and may volunteer with religious groups, while the young boys of the family may be members of the local cricket team. Another case in point can be Muslim or Christian families who identify very strongly with their mosque or church congregations and are members of book clubs and intellectual groups at universities, reading feminist and liberal texts. We become part of certain communities by default, given our social identities, but we can also choose to be part of several other communities that invite participation if our values and ideas align with their collective goals and ideology.

Our *primary communities* are those in which we gain membership mostly on the basis of our birth, because of our religion, caste, class and gender. Our primary communities are often extremely rigid and exclusive. Within these groups, members continue to reinforce the dominant belief systems and seldom engage with differences. It is also very easy to turn these communities into echo-chambers, and this can result in people developing myopic understanding about others. On the other hand, our *secondary communities* are those that we consciously choose to become members of because we relate to their work and values, or we enjoy doing certain activities together. These communities are flexible, more open to different ideas and people from different walks of life. In a way, secondary communities are more democratic in nature and aim to create non-hierarchical structures of organization. Some examples include literary societies, film clubs, activist groups, online communities with participants from many countries, political outfits, volunteer organizations, social welfare communities, sports clubs, online gaming communities, among others. In the first section of the chapter, we will focus mainly on understanding how primary communities can be made more liberal and inclusive. Towards the end of the chapter, we will enlist some secondary communities in which children can participate to further their personal, literary, political, professional and other life goals.

Interestingly, unlearning bias is as much a communication challenge as an ideological one.

Any form of belief is practised through channels of communication. These communication channels could be technological, personal, traditional, communal and so on. Imagine a tea stall at the entrance gate of a large residential complex, a public municipal water tap in towns, local trains in metropolitan cities, kitty parties and slumber parties. All of these places act as sites of communication and invite discussions on a diverse range of topics related to people's everyday lives. People use these sites to communicate their beliefs and biases. Within this context of communication, it is extremely easy to fall back into our echo-chambers, to circulate hatred and reinforce stereotypes at high speeds and to give priority to quantity over quality of information.

For instance, we are witnessing a global rise in cases of fake news, and this phenomenon has serious implications for information societies. The family/neighbourhood WhatsApp groups are a very interesting example of a community space where children are trained to uncritically respect the authority of their elders. Messages shared in these groups, the dialogues between adults and other 'community talks' are sometimes extremely rigid and oppressive. Parents often decide to submit to these dialogues and to participate without questioning anyone for fear of *log kya kahenge.*

These are some of the places and groups where we can begin our process of unlearning together. We must transform our communities, make them more inclusive and equal, convert them into safe spaces where values of compassion and justice are constantly practised in action, language and thought. Children partner with their parents to challenge the insensitivity towards differences that has been normalized in our communities. We must expand the boundaries of our compassion to include those outside our in-groups.

Let us look at some of the strategies that we can adopt to influence our communities.

STRATEGY I. FIND TACTFUL AND INNOVATIVE WAYS TO CHALLENGE STEREOTYPES

We need the courage to challenge our relatives and the elders in the community. What can we do to challenge friends and other community members, in a polite but firm manner, every time they pass a sexist joke or send messages with fake news or reprimand children from refusing to fall in line. Of course, we understand that you cannot pick up a fight every time someone posts a problematic message on WhatsApp, and that you cannot insult guests when you have invited them for dinner, but there are ways to challenge them tactfully. Ask a question, post or forward something that challenges their notions, use humour as a powerful weapon to oppose their views or share a personal story that might show a different perspective.

Some strategies to present counterpoints and narratives in such circles include the following:

- Use well-researched journalistic pieces that reflect your arguments and opinions on topics.
- Instead of rejecting their norms and traditions, try asking questions in ways that will highlight the gaps in their understanding.
- Be prepared to unlearn when presented with new facts and convincing arguments.
- Spend time writing down words and phrases that are non-confrontational and inclusive.
- Encourage your children to pay attention to and engage with these offensive dialogues respectfully instead of ignoring them or entering into communication deadlocks.
- Establish that disagreeing with other people's opinions and ideologies is not a sign of disrespect.
- Try to make our immediate communities more inclusive to avoid turning them into echo-chambers and social silos. Listen to and converse with people who are beyond our immediate community circles and invite them to be a part of our groups.
- Join diverse communities, online and offline.
- Practise compassion towards very senior members of groups who find it hard to fully comprehend progressive ideas and concepts that are radically new for them. It might be difficult to convince some old people that gender is a spectrum and that people should be allowed to practise gender fluidity. Introduce simple and easy-to-digest concepts and give them time to change. Even when they refuse to accept these new concepts, continue to engage with them and ask them questions to

understand their reservations and apprehensions about these new norms and practices.

STRATEGY II. COLLABORATING TO CHALLENGE DISCRIMINATION

An interesting way to challenge discrimination is to collaborate with people from different backgrounds for work, study and other activities. When we collaborate with others, it is important to ensure that everyone has an equal stake in the work processes— an equal voice in consensus building. People should be allowed to tell stories of their struggle in their own voice. Collaboration over study projects and team-building activities can also foster a sense of belonging and empathy towards others' life problems. An important condition in such activities is that we stop judging and start understanding other people's experiences.

In an interesting experiment that we conducted with rural school students in Gujarat, we got children to work in teams and create photo stories where Hindu and Muslim boys and girls were team members. It was very interesting to witness how gradually team members started looking at a person as a great photographer rather than a Muslim girl/boy and listened to someone's ideas on the basis of pure merit. They intimately came to know about their team members which challenged many of their preconceived notions of labels such a girl, boy, Hindu and Muslim.

Community neighbourhoods and spaces can be used for interesting collaborative work and projects. Collaboration over recreational, study or work projects has been identified as a very effective way of nurturing relationships between different groups. Can we think of different projects over which people from other communities can visit our neighbourhoods and collaborate with us? Communities can seek collaboration over social work, such as providing food to the homeless in the neighbourhoods, media consultation, educating children who live on streets, painting drab and dirty walls with attractive art and putting up an impromptu camp fire or an open mic night.

In the city of Vadodara (Gujarat), youth from a Hindu neighbourhood in Tarsali collaborated with Muslim youth from a neighbouring community to create a small group called 'Teaching on the Streets'. These young volunteers identified street corners around their community neighbourhoods and set up a classroom there every morning on Saturdays and Sundays to teach street children. Tasks related to planning and organizing were conducted on Wednesdays where youth from these two communities met, talked with each other and discussed their problems. This allowed them to know each other on the basis of 'common interests and motivations' and not on the basis of pre-existing differences. Trying to get familiar with others on the basis of shared interests and life goals is a very enriching experience and can help people transcend their biases and prejudices.

In yet another instance, media educators in Ahmedabad encouraged children from the Hindu and Muslim neighbourhoods in Ahmedabad to create interreligious study groups. These study groups were assigned a photography assignment. They were requested to visit each other's neighbourhoods, and to capture the cultural markers that defined the character of those places. As observed, Muslim students became tour guides for their Hindu teammates when the group was in a Muslim neighbourhood and introduced them to sites and symbols of importance in their community, such as the mosque, dargah, the paan shop, the playgrounds and other places. Similarly, Hindu students introduced their Muslim teammates to the temples they frequented, the vegetable market, the small shrines on the roads, the various rituals they performed on trees and other such places. The photo stories submitted by each group were extremely well thought out; they tried to bring together elements of both cultures and to create a beautiful tapestry of images symbolizing the coexistence of these religious groups in the city.

Personal experience with others can have both a liberating and a limiting effect. For instance, for Muslim youth who are already prejudiced against Hindus, one personal experience with a Hindu, who reinforces their prejudice, can push the Muslim youth further into the abyss of discrimination. It is easy to generalize and then to use personal anecdotes to substantiate these generalizations. On the other hand, when this experience with the other is positive, it can help both parties involved shed their biases and perceive the other party as friendly, kind or generous. If communities want to create positive collaborative spaces for intergroup engagements, they must ensure that

- The organizing committee that regulates these spaces should include young, old, men, women and all the different groups within the community.
- The committee weighs the risks involved in each project very critically.
- Every community member is aware of and encouraged to participate in these collaborative spaces, including in the decision-making process.
- Spaces and projects are conceptualized on the basis of 'common interests' of people from different sections.
- Meetings, discussions and other activities are held in neutral public spaces so that everyone feels comfortable participating.
- Grievances related to bullying, isolating, ignoring and suppressing are addressed with sensitivity and a sense of urgency.

STRATEGY III. PRACTISING CARE

Practising care includes using sensitive language and actions that do not stigmatize or ignore differences in our communities. We can start with preventing the segregation we practise within our communities—with domestic help, neighbours from different castes and religions, and those from underserved families and communities.

We can start with simple steps, such as inviting people from different backgrounds to our functions and making them feel welcomed. It is equally important to accept their invitations. We can also encourage young people to familiarize themselves with the lives of those who are different from us to better understand where other people are coming from and what their struggles are. Literature and films are great ways of experiencing people and life situations that we are not likely to encounter in our day-to-day lives. We can go a step ahead and also deliberately seek experiences such as volunteering, going on camps and participating in ecotourism.

Practising care and empathy is a skill that will be valuable in different facets of our lives. When children learn to enact care towards others, they develop a sense of right and wrong on the basis of universal principles of justice, dignity and equality.

Is it possible to erase years of socialization and suddenly develop empathy for others? No, expecting that you can undo your biases or dislike completely and quickly is expecting too much too soon. Also, sometimes you feel reluctant to immediately change your mind because you have had your own less-promising experiences with people.

In many instances, it seems impossible to develop empathy and love towards people from other castes and religious communities. In some of the interviews we conducted with people who had been victims of the Hindu–Muslim riots in Gujarat in 2002, many from both religions expressed that it was nearly impossible for them to start from a place of love or empathy while thinking about people from the other religion. Also, communities that have experienced continued hatred and domination from certain groups may develop a sense of hatred or anger towards these groups. How can we deal with these feelings of hatred, anger and prejudice, so that we may accept or at least tolerate others, if not love them?

Tolerance, we believe, is an important concept here. In situations where it is extremely painful to ignore differences or one's dislike for the other, tolerance teaches us three things: first, freedom and rights are not absolute. We cannot encroach on other's freedom in the process of asserting our liberties. Second, if freedom is not universal and guarantees rights to only a select few on the basis of their social identities, then it isn't freedom. It is prejudice in action. Third, change is a slow process because people are complicated and defined by layers of different life experiences.

Tolerance is a place of action—a non-judgemental approach towards differences in our societies. In political circles, tolerance is often used to mask indifference towards minorities, and we must be wary of such a usage of the term. Tolerance involves respecting different belief systems and lifestyles, cultivating an open mind, listening to competing opinions and recognizing and accepting plurality. That does not mean values such as human dignity, the value of life and the right to fulfil basic needs are negotiable. In contemporary times, tolerance has come to be recognized as a privilege enjoyed by the dominant group and a favour they extend towards other less privileged communities. The original and inclusive interpretation of the term is collapsing under the weight of the tension between what is proposed in theory and what is practised in our politics.

In the next strategy, we explain how tolerance can be practised in words and actions in relation to intergroup interactions and relationships.

STRATEGY IV. TALKING THROUGH OUR DIFFERENCES

We have observed in previous chapters that most of us prefer to remain confined to our echo-chambers and befriend those who support our views and opinions. This is definitely the easier path, if not an interesting or enriching one. It can be compared to the dilemma that we face in deciding whether to stick with an expressway or take a more scenic route. Most of us do not actively seek out people with different ideologies or initiate discussions and conversations with them.

Do you think that our societies would have experienced any real change if people had stopped exchanging ideas and opinions, however contentious the process may be? For instance, one of the most powerful reasons why India is less homophobic (accepting gay, lesbian, bisexual, transgender, intersex and asexual people) today than it was some 10 years ago is because people from the LGBTQIA community strived to create spaces where they could convey and express their experiences and ideas. When these new ideas reached people, there was an initial resistance, because people either chose not to understand or chose not to engage with the idea of homosexuality. Today, however, there is more acceptance and discussion around this issue. As we can see, there is a possibility of change, even if it is slow and grudging.

Why Conversations Are Important

The relationship between people and their communities is conversational in nature. The aim of conversations is not necessarily to come to agreements. Good conversation creates possibilities of steering through messy situations and conflicts without the use of aggression, hatred or violence. These conversations could be face to face or online. With regard to resolving conflicts, any conversation should have the following three core elements:

- First, the *language of care* wherein we indicate a sense of respect for all conversationalists and ensure that everyone has an equal stake in the process of speaking and listening.
- Second, the *tone of comfort* such that everyone feels included and heard.

- Third, *sensitive content* signalling a deep empathy for the experiences and realities of others.

Unlike the terms such as debates and discussions, the term 'conversations' is, in a sense, 'personal'. It involves an equilibrium between the people involved, as each person articulates their narratives and stories. Personalizing conversations related to conflicts can initiate in people a sense of connection and responsibility towards others. For instance, instead of discussing the problem of Islamophobia, if we turn towards the personal stories of our Muslim friend Fatima, our response to her own story of discrimination she has experienced will be more sympathetic and kinder. Our heart breaks when we hear first-hand our friend Anita talk about how difficult it was to 'come out as a woman' when her entire family wanted her to stay as Anil—a male identity Anita was given at birth. Conversations lay open the many ways in which these conflicts affect not some abstract notion of a specific community with a religious or caste label, but people we know— our friends, teachers, co-workers and neighbours. Also, when we try to learn about each other through conversations, we are willing to learn unique and novel things about them that will challenge existing stereotypes.

For a Muslim woman who was raised to believe that Hindus are violent and intolerant, conversations can be a great starting point to learn otherwise. Her interactions with Hindu women at her workplace may reveal that there are differences within the Hindu community. Some people are conservative and would choose not to associate with Muslims, while others may be warm and welcoming; some are vegetarian, while others devour biryani and kebabs. It leads to a realization that no community is a monolith and that there are many internal differences and novelties.

FRAMING: WHAT ARE YOU LOOKING AT?

A frame is like a window through which we look at a picture. If our window is wider, we take in more of the scene. Similarly, if we include historical narratives, present realities and future possibilities in our conversations, it allows for more space and complexity. For instance, in conversations with members from the ST/SC/OBC community on the quota system in India, if we consider how they have suffered systemic discrimination and marginalization and how high-caste privileges have been putting generations of others in an unfair situation in (public) life, we will find it easier to understand their demands to use and hold onto the reservation system in the country. At the same time, we will also be able to see how well-established and accomplished members from the group continue to take unfair advantage of the system.

Conversations are not so much about persuasion as about 'thinking through together'. They help us to establish harmonious relations with people who have different views and ideologies.

To understand how this is possible, let us draw an example from one of the episodes in the second season of an English original show called 'Skins'. In this episode, school boys—a gay English kid, a Muslim kid and a White English kid—are best friends. The Muslim kid invites his other two friends to his birthday party and promises that he will inform his parents that one of his friends is gay. At the party, however, he reveals that he has not been able to gather the courage to tell his Muslim parents that he has a gay friend. To this, the gay friend refuses to enter the house and stands at the gate. When the father comes to the door to resolve the issue, he invites the gay kid to the party even though his religion teaches him otherwise. The father explains that his faith is very important to him, and even when he goes to the mosque regularly, he cannot claim that he understands everything. The one thing he knows for sure is that the gay kid was his child's best friend and so he is welcome in the house. The Muslim father, in this case, chose to hold onto his belief without imposing his interpretation or morality onto others. Many people may criticize this approach as relativism, but we interpret it as a method of sitting with differences without translating them into acts of unkindness or hatred. What the father did was accept that his religion teaches him that homosexuality is wrong, but that he will not practise it by being unkind and cruel to someone else.

Why Rock the Boat?

The act of inviting differences to a common table through shared conversations is tricky, often risky and even dangerous many a times. We might wonder, why rock the boat? What if I am in a difficult situation because everyone else around me does not support my humanist views? It is often believed that anything that is unknown, remote and alien is necessarily evil and ominous. To cultivate this fear, our society often punishes those who are seen as venturing outside the community boundary. It is a strategy to maintain loyalty and adherence to community norms.

Instead of being afraid, if we continue initiating contact and conversations with others, we will push ourselves to have an open mind and be prepared to engage with differences. Both authors have spent several years abroad, getting our doctoral degrees, and have lived in these foreign countries for various purposes. Our lives would not have been so rich if people in those countries had not opened their doors to us. Also, if we had not shown the willingness to accept their invitation, to be part of their cultures, we would have missed out on a lot of learning opportunities.

STRATEGY V. PRACTISING TOLERANCE IN OUR COMMUNITIES

How often do we survey our neighbourhoods and streets to examine how our communities are positioned in relation to others? For instance, have we ever paid attention to how residential areas and public spaces in our cities are often segregated on the basis of religion, caste, class and gender identities? Many cities, such as Vadodara, Ahmedabad, Delhi, Lucknow, Calcutta, Bangalore and others, have a very noticeable division between Hindu and Muslim neighbourhoods. Hindu families and residents purchase houses and live exclusively in Hindu-dominated areas, whereas Muslims stay in separate neighbourhoods. Also, the poor Dalits and several lower caste communities occupy separate residential areas in the cities, often removed or sent away from the houses of the upper caste and class. Similarly, underserved transgenders, often referred to as hijras, are thrown out of the families they are born into and adopted by other hijras who live in clearly marked neighbourhoods. We have so much diversity, and instead of allowing these differences to seep into one other, we have cordoned them in neat watertight boxes.

Practising tolerance in our communities begins with identifying how different tactics are used to keep certain groups out. Lower caste people and women are not allowed to enter certain places or participate in some religious functions. Poor people are refused entry into multi-storey entertainment and shopping malls because their clothes and demeanour do not match the class requirements normalized by mall owners/goers. Dark-skinned students are not given an opportunity to present bouquets to the chief guest. These obvious practices of discrimination raise questions such as: why do we do this? Do we discriminate against others unthinkingly, because that is how it has always been? How do we change this? On the basis of our work in different communities, we have enlisted a few strategies to increase representation and diversity in our communities.

1. *Letting all voices be heard:* Many of our primary communities are controlled and organized by a generation of older people, especially men, who are often scared of change and constructive tension. For instance, in various religious congregations, older men take the responsibility of making rules and guidelines for everyone. They also assume the authority of counselling, sometimes coaxing or scolding members into following community rules. Have you observed something similar in the organizing committee in your apartment building or residential society that largely consists of older men who often refuse to invite the participation or opinions of others? Similarly, in women-dominated groups, older women normally assume the charge and leadership. As it is, in India, we respect age, and women are taught to stay silent when men speak. Such practices and teachings create a hierarchy in our primary communities, and marginal voices, especially those of children, youth and women are rarely heard. Their voices are especially silenced if they try to challenge the norms or suggest an option. Let us look at the following example.

In a very affluent residential building in the city of Vadodara, a young female college student invited some of her friends (girls and boys) to play table tennis in her apartment's common playroom. When the watchman saw this group of boys and girls playing together in the afternoon, he asked them to leave the table tennis room under the pretext that outsiders were not allowed. This reason was untrue because the society guidelines did not have this reason listed as a clause of compliance. When the matter was examined closely, it was revealed that the watchman was instructed by older men who were a part of the apartment's council committee to bar young girls from playing and spending time with boys without adult supervision. As is obvious, this was a case of moral policing and the young female resident was extremely upset.

In this situation, it would be very effective to make the organizing and council committee more diverse and to include children, young members and women in decision-making processes. Every day, we come across instances where our children suggest something new and we refuse to consider their suggestions seriously because we think that children and young adults are not mature enough to contribute in meaningful ways. Similarly, in clubs and caste-based organizations, the wealthier a person (again, mostly a man), the more say he would have. Why do we believe that if someone has more money, he or she will also always have the brightest idea and the most appropriate suggestions?

This must change. Our communities must be representative of different voices, opinions and ideas. We must provide those who are normally silent, either because they have no authority, or because they are in a minority, or because they are considered outsiders and different, with equal opportunities to speak and be heard. In a madrasa or church, for instance, young children and adolescents should have the right to question the authority on the authenticity of religion and the concept of a single God. They should be included in discussions on how to change and update internal administration in mosques and churches, encouraged to deliver public speeches which address the concerns of our contemporary plural societies and allowed to ideate projects for community service and outreach. Similarly, a young girl should be allowed to question unnecessary restrictions imposed on her during her menstrual cycle, or a Hindu boy should be allowed to issue objections if his Muslim or Dalit friends are served food separately.

2. *Making our communities accessible to outsiders:* At the Sabarmati Ashram in Ahmedabad, scholars of different religions are invited regularly to highlight how their religions talk about peace and tolerance. After the scholar has given a talk or staged a performance, the audience is invited to raise questions, provide insightful comments and share their experiences. The audience comprises people from different classes, castes, genders and religious communities. The Sabarmati Ashram and various other organizations that promote intergroup dialogue and engagement use the Gandhian philosophies to make sites and spaces accessible and democratic. Some of these guidelines include granting equal representation and authority to everyone participating, avoiding the use of violence or aggression in words or actions, cultivating listening skills and practising respect.

We can use these guidelines to make our communities accessible to outsiders. Encouraging community members to invite their friends, relatives or colleagues from different socio-economic backgrounds for community events and to make acquaintances with in-group members can be a liberating experience.

Let us consider a possible scenario in which we realize that some members in our community belong to the LGBTQIA group but are scared to discuss it with others. Every religious community will have conservative followers who refuse to accept that gender and sexuality is a spectrum. Many religious leaders are not willing to accept LGBTQIA people. People who rely only on a singular interpretation of their religion might find the idea unacceptable. In this case, members of the community can suggest inviting people to conduct workshops or informal sessions to initiate conversations on gender sensitivity, equality and rights without creating pressure on others to immediately change their views. Most importantly, members from LGBTQIA organizations should be included among the speakers. Although such workshops and sessions will be uncomfortable for some people within the community, it will give them a new perspective to consider. Such workshops and sessions can also be very insightful for those members who identify themselves as LGBTQIA but are too scared to come out of the closet.

Another way to make these spaces accessible to everyone is the technique of sharing power. The authority of organizing and approving events in the community should be shared by different people. Positions of power must be assigned on a rotation basis. Include everyone to participate in the process of decision-making occasionally. This will ensure that more people with different values and ideas can express their concerns.

Finally, to make these spaces accessible to outsiders, try and build connections with different communities through collaborative activities. For instance, frequent different places of worship in small groups and learn about the different religious rituals performed there. Of course, we must make sure we do not behave like careless tourists. Walking into a gurdwara will introduce people to the values of serving others and piety, the time spent in a mosque will teach us the power of discipline in life and worship and participating in an *aarti* at a temple can make us realize the effects of devotional music and meditation. At the Sabarmati Ashram, for instance, interfaith prayer ceremonies are held every day. Frequenting such gatherings can be a starting point towards introducing in-group members to ideas of coexistence and allowing them to engage with more people. Also, exposure to people from other regions, countries, ages, interests and political views goes a long way in initiating the practice of critical thinking.

3. *Creating opportunities to help older generation unlearn their biases:* The older generation—our parents, grandparents and community elders—finds it harder to let go off their biases and prejudices. As people age, they often develop a sense of loss,

they feel that they are losing authority, power and control over the new generation. This is completely natural and normal. In this phase, community elders cling very tightly onto their old traditions and customs, even when doing so is against socio-economic development and positive change. Let us take the example of Khap Panchayats in India. In many articles about the role of Khap Panchayats,[1-3] three things have become evident.

- Most of these Khaps have leaders who are male, aged 60 years or above and who are retired.
- Most of these leaders have an authoritative approach and refuse to consider opinions of young people or women.
- They often use extreme forms of punishment, including but not limited to beating, public humiliation, social ostracization and sometimes death (killing through lynching) as acceptable ways of disciplining community members. All this is done on the pretext of saving the honour of the community.

Such elders create a sense of fear among the community that younger generations will lose their values and traditions if they are not coaxed into following the rules established by their ancestors decades or generations ago. Such fear mongering allows community elders to impose harsh punishments, and they are seldom held accountable for their actions.

[1] S. Makkar, 'Panchayats under the Shadow of the "Khaps"' (2013). Available at https://www.livemint.com/Politics/nW03eT80k8lmHDfAUGh33J/Panchayats-under-the-shadow-of-the-khaps.html (accessed on 21 January 2021).

[2] J. Sangwan, 'Khap Panchayat: Signs of Desperation? (2010). Available at https://www.thehindu.com/opinion/lead/Khap-panchayat-signs-of-desperation/article13796344.ece (accessed on 21 January 2021).

[3] S. Thapar-Björkert, 'If There Were No Khaps [...] Everything Will Go Haywire [...] Young Boys and Girls Will Start Marrying into the Same Gotra': Understanding Khap-Directed "Honour Killings" in Northern India', in 'Honour' Killing and Violence (London: Palgrave Macmillan, 2014). A. K. Gill, C. Strange, K. Roberts (eds). Available at: https://doi.org/10.1057/9781137289568_8

As adults who support a more democratic environment, we can try a few tactics.

- Help create community spaces where everyone can express their opinions in a respectful manner. No one should feel threatened or bullied because they hold different opinions.
- Question and challenge when members are punished for their personal decisions related to their choice in marriage partners, food habits, lifestyle practices, among others.
- Ensure a system where authority changes hands and no one can hold a position of power for a long time. Encourage some like-minded members to advocate that everyone has the right to claim access to positions of power and resource distribution.

Unlearning, especially for older generations, can be a challenging task. First, they do not have unrestricted access to informational resources, like the young generation does. Second, their exposure is limited to community interactions. They seldom go to places where everyone has equal access and say. They do not frequent public places very often. Third, given how they are raised, they find it very difficult to apologize, and they also have the fear of losing authority and control. Not being needed anymore, being obsolete or irrelevant is the fear that many older people face, especially when they have had a long stint in a position of authority, either at work or at home. Instead of blaming our elders for intellectual stagnation, a more effective approach can be to ensure that they have access to information, resources and perspectives from beyond their comfort zone.

- Work with your children to educate your parents and older relatives about fake news when they send you a false message on WhatsApp or other social media.
- Respectfully call out the racism, colourism, anti-Muslim/Hindu/other religious sentiments, hatred towards lower caste

groups, body shaming or slut shaming instances in group chats and family discussions.

- Make your organizations truly intergenerational. Encourage elders to participate in community services in their free time; put them in touch with organizations where they can meet people from different backgrounds.
- If our elders are mistreating domestic helps or sanitary workers, call it out without being harsh or rude. Request them to be more sensitive and kinder towards others.
- Spend some time with your elders watching or reading narratives that challenge discriminatory social norms in our societies.

Watch and read these with the elders.

Movies	Books
1. *Court*, directed by Chaitanya Tamhane	1. *Behind the Beautiful Forevers: Life, Death, and Hope in a Mumbai Undercity* by Katherine Boo
2. *Article 15*, directed by Anubhav Sinha	2. *Everybody Loves a Good Drought* by P. Sainath
3. *Sairat*, directed by Nagraj Manjule	3. *Poor Economics* by Abhijit Banerjee and Esther Duflo
4. *My Brother... Nikhil*, directed by Onir	4. *Seeing Like a Feminist* by Nivedita Menon
5. *Revolutionary Optimists* by Maren Garinger-Monsen and Nicole Newnham	5. *Family Matters* by Rohinton Mistry
6. *Pataal Lok*, directed by Avinash Arun and Prosit Roy	6. *Coolie* by Mulk Raj Anand

Movies	Books
7. *Thappad*, directed by Anubhav Sinha	7. *My Friend, My Enemy: Essays, Reminiscences, Portraits* by Ismat Chughtai
8. *Peepli Live*, directed by Anusha Rizvi and Mahmood Farooqui	8. *Why Loiter? Women and Risk on Mumbai Streets* by Shilpa Phadke, Sameera Khan and Shilpa Ranade
9. *Masaan*, directed by Neeraj Ghaywan	9. *Unaccustomed Earth* by Jhumpa Lahiri
10. *Nil Batte Sanata*, directed by Ashwiny Iyer Tiwari	10. *The Ministry of Utmost Happiness* by Arundhati Roy

Practising tolerance at home, in schools and in our communities is not a one-time commitment. Begin small, stay local and constantly update. There are many ways in which we can contribute towards building a peaceful and tolerant society, and there is no one right way.

Unlearning is a slow process. Some are questioning gender roles at home, some are writing articles and blogs, and yet others are protesting in the public square. Some are initiating difficult conversations with their families, while others are changing policies. Some are filing public interest litigations, while others are creating awareness in their neighbourhoods and communities. Although our ways are many and different, what matters is that we do not lose sight of our goal of creating an inclusive, peaceful society and continue to strive towards it.

CHAPTER 6

It Isn't Real,
It Is Photoshopped!

What do your children watch, read, listen and follow for fun?

If you are thinking that we are prompting you to snoop on your children's media use, that is not our purpose at all! We want you to be aware of the kind of media content your children consume and also what they produce.

REFLECTIVE EXERCISE I

What is entertainment media? How will you describe entertainment media such as popular songs, films, television shows and celebrities? Let us look at the following list of words and select the ones that apply to our definition of entertainment media.

Act	Creation	Artificial
Story	Glamorous	Fiction
Real	Constructed	Entertaining
Ethical	Morality	Lens
Depressing	Exaggerated	Technology

Now spend some time jotting down your definition of entertainment media. What can you draw from your everyday experiences? Which shows, movies and songs do your family watch for entertainment? Why are these shows and movies entertaining? What do they do? How do your children entertain themselves using media? What is their media diet?

Entertainment media are media created and consumed for the purposes of entertainment, leisure and relaxation. Although these media are created for the sole purpose of entertaining audiences, they form a large portion of our everyday media diets. Entertainment media can consist of a huge range of media formats as well as media habits. To begin with, popular Bollywood and Hollywood movies, albums and songs, radio programmes, television shows, and online games are all forms of media created for entertainment purposes. These media are channelled through television, cinema halls, radios, Internet-based sources and mobile phones. It is interesting to observe how the use of the Internet and mobile phones has increased the scope of the entertainment media. We can now access international shows and movies on various online platforms such as Netflix, Hulu, Amazon Prime, HBO and others. This new entertainment environment has changed our media habits, especially among young people. Nowadays, besides watching shows, movies and songs, young people spend considerable time following, reading, watching and engaging with celebrities and their online pages on Facebook, Instagram, Twitter and other social media platforms. The practice of scrolling, reading stories, watching vlogs (video logs), posting and commenting are all part of the young generation's media diet for entertainment and leisure. In such a dynamic environment, where the lines between the real and the fictional worlds are blurred, young people are increasingly influenced by what they see and watch in the media. Many young people mimic celebrities, social media influencers and the culture promoted by the media. Also, a large number of media are produced to make money and therefore they do not like to challenge or displease people. Most popular media are produced keeping the audience appeal in mind and not with an intention of bringing about social change. So if they can create humour or sex appeal or drama by pandering to stereotypes, they will not try to change their products and narratives. These products, however, can leave lasting impressions on young minds.

SANJANA AND HER STRUGGLES WITH BODY IMAGE

Sanjana is an 18-year-old college student. She has just started a relationship with her first boyfriend, Niraj. Sanjana and Niraj are both huge fans of Bollywood. Sanjana tries very hard to model her behaviour, looks and appearance after Bollywood actresses as she knows that Niraj finds it attractive. She is in awe of their lifestyles as portrayed through the social media pages of these actresses on Facebook and Instagram.

Sanjana uses many photo editing software to lighten her photos, to remove blemishes on her skin and to look thinner in the pictures she posts of herself, especially her photos with Niraj. In our conversations, she explained how she uses specific camera angles to make sure she looks thinner. Niraj constantly compares her with models and actresses. Sanjana follows a strict diet, and her mother complains that she often starves herself. Her college counsellor has diagnosed that she suffers from negative body image. She does not feel confident in her body—she thinks she is fat, does not have a perfect skin and has ugly features.

In our conversations, she often said she would get some cosmetic surgeries done when she grows up—she wants to enlarge her breasts, desires a liposuction around her waist and wants to get a laser hair removal treatment done. She uses a lot of fairness creams, face masks and other products to lighten her skin tone and to acquire the perfect skin. She often refuses to go to social gatherings when she feels bloated and ugly. She has lost interest in academics, extracurricular activities and sports. She thinks that playing sports will tan her skin and make her look bad. Worst of all, she is constantly insecure about Niraj leaving her if she does not fit the media-created image of a beautiful woman.

The term body image is defined as our perception of our physical appearance, that is, how we look, feel and think about our bodies. Young people's body images are greatly influenced by the media they consume. In our conversations with Sanjana, we asked her why she wanted to lighten her skin tone. She said:

Who would want to marry a dark girl? You think you cannot
do anything about the skin tone but that is wrong. All I need
is some expertise and money. Look at all the actresses—
Deepika, Priyanka, Ileana, and others. All of them were dark
and like the girls-next-door when they entered the industry.
Now, they are fair. That is because they invest time and
money in their skin and bodies. I can get a lighter skin tone
if I take care of my skin.

As she says this, she pulls out a Fair and Lovely tube from her
purse and describes her skincare routine.

A dermatologist from Ahmedabad discussed this obsession
with fairness cream among young people in India.

Young people watch these celebrities endorse fairness creams
all the time. These advertisements insist that if people are not
fair, they cannot be successful, good looking, or impressive.
Then they see these actresses on their Instagram handles or
in movies and shows without realizing that they photoshop
the images to make sure that the 'glam quotient' remains
intact. So young people are being raised on a diet of glossed,
photoshopped, and artificial beauty standards. The tags such
as #summerbody, #bikinibody, #bodygoals are often trending
on Instagram with millions of posts and followers. They
develop unrealistic expectations from themselves—they want
to wake up and look like the actresses look after seven layers of
makeup and perfect camera lighting. They also have unrealistic
expectations for their romantic partners. Girls, of course, have
much more pressure to look a certain way than boys but the
media also make boys insecure about their bodies. In recent
years, my clinic has witnessed an increase in younger patients
who want to change something about their body—they hate
how they look naturally. This is troublesome for a simple
reason that their ideas about 'the perfect body' are unattainable

and in order to achieve these goals they harm themselves. They will starve, apply a lot of harmful products and chemicals, go for unnecessary surgeries such as breast enlargement or nose-jobs and so on. Parents do not know better, and in some cases even encourage their children to go for such measures.

Going even a step further, when a certain skin colour or physical appearance is given more than due attention, qualified candidates suffer in job interviews, talented artists fail to get due recognition for their talents and people even end up choosing a wrong life partner! Media plays a huge role in creating an image of an ideal man or an ideal woman.

Media messages are amplified by people in our surroundings: our parents, friends, families, teachers and neighbours. They often taunt and humiliate young people with dark skin and make them feel less beautiful, attractive and impressive. In our work as media educators, we have experienced many instances where children felt they were not cast in lead roles for school drama and stage activities because of how they look. In most of these cases, fair, tall and slim students were cast as protagonists or lead dancers, even if other students had better dancing, acting and other skills. Similarly, in our families and neighbourhoods, we have often seen elders tease young people if they are fat, have acne, dark skin and often extend unsolicited advice. Let us look at the following story submitted by a 26-year-old man.

I was rejected in school and college for being dark-skinned, and I remember buying men's fairness cream to treat this. Today, I am mature, and I have learned to embrace my body, but those remarks still lower my self-confidence sometimes. I still do not feel confident wearing a white shirt because my mum used to say that white colour makes me look darker. She advised me to wear colour tones that would not contrast with my skin colour. Our parents and relatives consume the same media and they believe in the very same ideas. My classmates used to call me *Kaalia, Kale, Chaprasi, Bhoot* and various other names. During my 12th grade, each student was supposed to have a date for the prom night; we were supposed to ask out the girls we liked. You will not believe this but I thought to myself, 'I will ask the ugliest girl out because I am ugly too and if she is uglier than me probably no one else will ask her so she won't turn me down.' Turns out, even she turned me down for a fairer guy. Now this is so wrong. I was bullied because of my skin tone, and I used the same unrealistic beauty standards to judge my female classmates. These ideal beauty standards are very toxic. It is a vicious cycle.

Young people derive their ideas about body, looks and self-image from their media and societies. Let us reflect on the following: which adjectives do you use to describe your children? Do you use any pet names for your children mocking their physical features, such as small eyes, chubby cheeks, plum bodies, heavy thighs, thin hair or rounded bellies? Have you heard other parents, elders, relatives, siblings and friends refer to young people as *tingu* (for short height), *takli* (for thin or short hair), *andhi* (if they wear spectacles), *jadi/moti/padi/hippo/bhains* (if they have heavy body type), *kali/kagadi/kolsa* (for dark skin tone) and other such abuses and slurs? Have you heard your family members crack jokes about young people's body type, physical attributes and looks? Have you advised your children to lose/gain some weight just to look attractive, or use face masks and creams to reduce the tan and brighten the skin, or expected them to work out excessively?

If your answer for any of these questions is 'yes', it means that our children and young people are being raised in an environment that promotes negative body image and may cause detrimental effects on their emotions, psyche and well-being. Let us spend some time on the following reflective exercise.

REFLECTIVE EXERCISE II

1. Sit down with a pen and a piece of paper.
2. Enlist five instances when you have, intentionally or unintentionally, said something that would contribute to your children's negative self-image.
3. Now, ask your children to define and describe an image they would like to cultivate about themselves.
4. Enlist the steps you can take in your everyday interactions to ensure that your children practise a positive self-image.
5. Create a chart to trace progress. Some indicators can be as follows: how many affirmative terms and phrases you used to boost your child's self-image? Which adjectives did you use to compliment, tease or describe your children? What is your children's response to these words of positivity? Did you ask your children how they are feeling about their bodies and their self?

This is not to say that we should always praise our children, even when they do not deserve to be praised. Your criticism, even if it is valid, should always be constructive. It should build the child's personality and confidence, not break them.

In the following section, we explain how the linkages between media and people's life experiences create insecurities, doubts and anxieties about their bodies and appearances. We also highlight how the media and society capitalize on people's insecurities to generate more revenue, customers and brand desirability for products.

CAPITALIZING ON YOUNG PEOPLE'S INSECURITIES

Companies manufacturing cosmetics, technologies, clothes and accessories, and various services tap into young people's insecurities to market their products and earn profits. Let us take the example of cameras with filters in our mobile phones. For many people, the most important criterion while choosing a phone is if cameras in the phone have a 'beauty mode'. This beauty mode allows people to lighten their skin, remove freckles, make their skin look flawless and sometimes make them look thin in their photos. Young people are often insecure about their looks, appearances and their bodies. Marketers and companies exploit these insecurities as they create a need for products that will help young people to temporarily alleviate their anxieties. In doing this, they reinforce their insecurities. Not only that, insecure people unknowingly impose these unreasonable standards on others and the vicious cycle of discrimination continues.

The 'beauty mode' in our phones allows adolescents to have a flawless and white skin in their photos. In including this feature, mobile companies justify and support young people's desire for fair and perfect skin, a thin body and expensive clothes. These materialistic desires and unrealistic expectations from our bodies also manifest themselves in the form of a lot of services and products that we buy every day—high-end expensive salons, gyms, clinics and nutritionists who guarantee a weight reduction of 10 kg in 3 weeks, clothes that make people look thinner such as tummy tuckers, online services and apps for beauty tips. Companies, media and the market anchor their messages on people's insecurities and create a societal pressure among young people to walk in line with normalized beauty standards in their societies.

Many luxury brands such as Dior, Versace, Louis Vuitton and others market their products as an aspirational value, that is, people who can afford to own these products are seen as successful and have a high social prestige. Let us look at the experiences shared by a young boy in Mumbai who was obsessed with normalized beauty standards.

OF BRANDS AND MONEY

I belong to a middle-class family. My parents are bankers, and they work really hard to ensure that my sister and I have a good education. They got us into an international school in Mumbai. Most of my classmates belonged to affluent families: the super-rich families, where parents spend very little time with their children and to compensate for that they buy them very expensive branded products. That was the time *Student of the Year* was also released, and it was very popular among people of my age. Girls would want to be like Shanaya and buy all branded products like Gucci and all. Girls who could not afford to buy these products or expensive clothes were bullied. They were called *behenji* and all.

Being poor or even middle class was a stigma, and to avoid that you had to show that you were rich. I started pestering my parents for more money. I was always insecure about my looks. I am dark and short. I thought, nobody wants to be with dark and short guys. I started buying very expensive and branded clothes to look more appealing. When my parents refused to buy me things, I stole money from their cupboards.

I was insecure, and everyone around me made me believe that I could buy my way out of insecurities. To be honest, that is not true. Your insecurities will only make you more vulnerable. To address your insecurities, you have to work on them. My mother compelled me to attend school counselling sessions because she knew about my insecurities. I was always an intelligent student, but all I cared about was how I looked and if I had enough money to 'fit in' and 'flaunt'. Counselling helped me a lot. I realized that my worth was more than what society had put on me. I was good at studies, I was good at sports and I loved reading. I always had something interesting to share and say.

I also started reading a lot of inspiring books. *Wings of Fire: An Autobiography of Abdul Kalam* by Abdul Kalam is still my favourite.

Teenage years can be messy. Many parents complain that when their children enter their teenage years, they distance themselves from their parents. They do not share everything with them. This also makes it difficult for parents to understand what is going on in the lives of their children. In many cases of bullying at school, parents say that they had no idea that their child was suffering or was being bullied. This is a phase when young people develop a sense of independence, confidence and exploration. They are curious about who they are, what they can achieve and if they can make decisions on their own.

As parents, this is also a transition phase for us. How do we tread the boundary between granting them autonomy and guiding them? How can we set limits to the level of independence that our children get to enjoy? And, most importantly, how do we monitor what children are watching, listening, talking and experiencing without undue interference and snooping?

Adolescence is a phase that renders young people vulnerable to a lot of societal pressures, especially the expectations set by their peer groups. As a result, they succumb to the norm more easily and conform to societal expectations. To fit into their group of friends, girls may start using a lot of make-up even if they do not like it, they may start going to the gym and diet, and they may even go on dates with people they do not like or appreciate. Many young people suffer from body issues when they are in their teens. To make this situation worse, young people spend a lot of time on social media and are constantly exposed to filtered images of influencers, celebrities and their friends.

It is difficult to encourage teenagers to challenge stereotypes, discriminatory norms and unfair practices because they want to be accepted, feel loved and to be included in their friend circles, school communities and neighbourhoods. If we want our children to stand up for what they believe is right, we will have to be parents and teachers who support them in this difficult task.

In India, very few schools have a 'media education' curriculum designed to equip young people with the critical skills required to understand that media images, stories and posts can be cleverly constructed, are artificial and not a reality even for those who create them. Let us understand the role of the media in shaping self and body image among young people and in reinforcing stereotypes.

MEDIA AS THE 'LOOKING GLASS SELF'

According to the theory of 'looking glass self', individuals develop a sense of self on the basis of how they believe others perceive them. People use social interaction as a 'mirror' to understand their position, image and worth in society. According to the sociologist Charles Cooley, self-concept is built in relation with others, in society and through conversations, rather than in solitude.

THE THREE STAGES OF THE 'LOOKING GLASS SELF' THEORY

Stage 1

In social situations, individuals learn to imagine how they appear to others.

Stage 2

Individuals imagine how other people judge their appearances on the basis of various cues.

Stage 3

Individuals develop a self-concept on the basis of their understanding of the judgement of others about their appearance.

We imagine how we appear to other people.

We imagine how other people judge the appearance that we think we present.

If we think the evaluation is favorable, our self-concept is enhanced.

If we think the evaluation is unfavorable, our self-concept is diminished.

In contemporary times, social media, for instance, is the most interesting example of a looking glass self. Every time we upload a photo, story or post on our social media profiles, we invite others to respond, react and judge our appearances and looks. Sometimes, the number of likes or comments is a sign of societal approval. When many people like or comment on our stories and photos, it reflects that our friends and followers approve of how we look and present ourselves. The same social media can be used to bully others and reject their value or worth. Most young people experience instances of cyberbullying and trolling through social media at least once in their lives. Similarly, they use their social media to create an image for themselves. They post about the things they like to do, the products they possess, where they live, what they eat and where they travel. All of these posts and stories are ways of entering into situations of social interactions and of trying to understand if our peers, relatives or followers reinforce our self-concept.

Young people have unlimited access to media technologies, platforms and channels. They spend a considerable amount of time on the media, and their realities are greatly shaped by their media usage. As the media is ubiquitous, it is tricky to identify blurring lines between the media and reality. We look very different from our heavily filtered, photoshopped and edited photographs. The imagined world of social media starts encroaching on our real lives. When young people cannot look at the way they appear on their social media, they feel anxious, less confident and 'ugly'.

In our conversations with young boys from a school in Vadodara, one student said:

> It would be so much fun if we all could look the way we do on social media. We could do whatever we want to with our faces—make the pimples and acne go away, get rid of the tan, and look super fair. I want to look like I look on my Instagram profile. I wish I were like these Bollywood actors. They are ripped. They look perfect even at home. They #wakeuplike that.

Media creates beauty myths. Popular media decide which type of body, facial features, skin and hair are acceptable and which are not. Our children's media diet influences their everyday habits, self-concept and self-worth. Not only that, these form the basis for judging and discriminating against those who don't fit this perfect picture. In the next section, we debunk some of these media myths and help our readers understand how to encourage children to have a healthy media diet.

DEBUNKING MEDIA MYTHS

Social media, Bollywood and our society are pressuring young people to attach their worth solely to how close they fit the bill of an 'ideal body type'. As adults, we have failed at creating a sense of respect and love for different body types among our younger generation and a passion for fitness over 'thinness' or 'six packs'. Their intelligence matters, their skills matter, their hobbies matter and their humane qualities matter most, but we are willing to ignore all of these in favour of looks. The media has only fuelled this anxiety. Our media has failed to represent different body types in stories, songs and events. In most Bollywood movies, the female protagonist is a fair and skinny actress with flawless skin, while the male protagonist is tall and handsome with a ripped body and six packs. Back in 2008, Kareena Kapoor flaunted the 'size zero' figure in the movie *Tashan* and many young girls started going on crash diets and worked out excessively to achieve that figure. Even today, 'a thigh gap' is a body goal for many young girls and women. As Kareena Kapoor's 'zero figure' became a popular desire among young girls, the fame of nutritionist Rujuta Diwekar grew. Diwekar published the book *Don't Lose Your Mind, Lose Your Weight* and with this came the era of new diets, gyming extensively, always being critical of one's body and never feeling at home. She tried to correct this myth with her later videos and books, but the 'size zero' aspiration stayed in public imagination. On top of that, the media is rampant with before and after weight-loss stories of celebrities such as Sonam Kapoor, Alia Bhatt, Sara Ali Khan and Sonakshi Sinha.

Although nutritionists and celebrities say that they support a healthy lifestyle and would want their followers and fans to not have any body issues, they often promote 'a thin fair body' as an ideal beauty standard. Phrases such as 'weight loss', 'skin treatments', 'shredding', 'dieting' and 'cosmetic procedures' have now become part of our common parlance. The number of cosmetic surgeries taking place in our country today is shocking. According to the International Society of Aesthetic Plastic Surgery, India ranks fourth in the world with 895,896 cosmetic procedures conducted in 2018.[1] Young people participate in all these activities in some capacity; they feel compelled to have diet plans and to lose weight, to look appealing and to be accepted. This can result in several eating disorders and cause trauma to the mind and body.

ANOREXIA AND BULIMIA: WHEN FOOD BECOMES AN ENEMY

In India, over 35 per cent of teenagers suffer from either of these eating disorders. The two most common forms of eating disorders among young people are bulimia and anorexia. Bulimia nervosa is an eating disorder characterized by periods of binge eating followed by either purging or over-exercising. In a study[2] conducted by a group of psychologists and psychiatrists, young people who belong to families which emphasize the need for staying in shape are more prone to suffering from bulimia nervosa. Popular culture and our media have promoted ideas such as 'thin is beautiful' and 'thigh gaps are sexy'. As a result, many young people now exercise more while refusing to eat healthy.

---

[1] ISAPS, *ISAPS International Survey on Aesthetic/Cosmetic Procedures Performed in 2018* (2018). Available at https://www.isaps.org/wp-content/uploads/2019/12/ISAPS-Global-Survey-Results-2018-new.pdf (accessed on 8 May 2020).

[2] Bárbara C. Machado, Sónia F. Gonçalves, Carla Martins, Isabel Brandão, António Roma-Torres, Hans W. Hoek and Paulo P. Machado, 'Anorexia Nervosa versus Bulimia Nervosa: Differences Based on Retrospective Correlates in a Case-control Study'. *Eating and Weight Disorders-Studies on Anorexia, Bulimia, and Obesity* 21, no. 2 (2016): 181–197.

Anorexia nervosa is another eating disorder increasingly diagnosed among young people, where individuals refuse to eat food and often starve themselves to lose weight. These eating disorders can lead to several nutritional deficiencies and defects in young people. Adolescence is an age where individuals must have a healthy intake of calcium and protein-rich foods to build up their bone mass. Bone health in adolescence is linked to bone health in later ages and, because of eating disorders, young people following these 'fad diets' are likely to have serious bone-related problems when they are older. If they follow strict diets and deprive themselves of nutrients, they may also be prone to detrimental hormonal changes and, in some cases, even heart damage and failure. When mother, cousins, aunts and other adult women in their social circle reinforce myth of 'looks are everything for a girl', there is no escaping from the beauty trap.

The media does not adequately highlight the effects of crash diets, harmful fairness creams or other toxic products created and marketed to promote ideal beauty standards. Consuming media uncritically can ruin young people's relation with food, their bodies and their minds. How can we expect our children to accept their bodies when the only kinds of bodies they watch and see on their screens are photoshopped, thin/lean and fair? How can we expect our children to be self-confident when the media and society fail to acknowledge diversity in the way people look, dress and present themselves? Should we hope that girls and boys will be confident in their own skin when the media, celebrities and influencers constantly animate the notions that

Fair is→Attractive
Slim is→Desirable
Curvy is→Sexy
Six Pack is→Hot
Smooth Skin is→Desirable

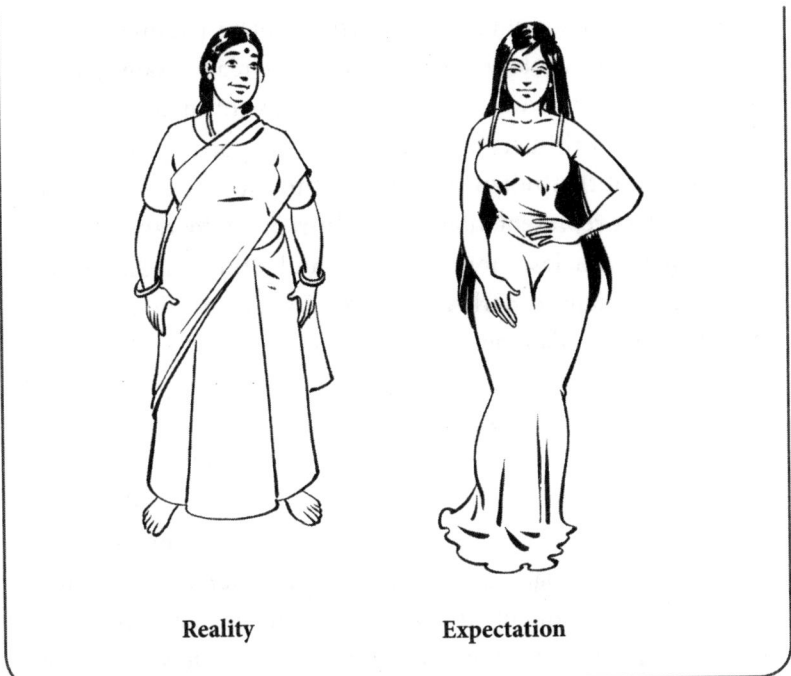

Reality   **Expectation**

How can we encourage our children to unpack the biases and insecurities built into these media products? How can we teach our children to love their bodies, to respect different skin tones and to develop a positive attitude towards their bodies and self? In the following section, we discuss this with an example of how parents and teachers can debunk the media myth of 'fair is lovely'.

DARK IS BEAUTIFUL

According to a 2018 report by Quartz, the global skin-lightening market is worth more than 10 billion dollars and aggressively peddles fairness products to people, especially in Asia and Africa. Before we start thinking of ways to challenge this skin-based racial discrimination we witness all around us, it is critical to examine the roots of this problem. Both Asia and Africa have been former colonies; many countries in these continents were ruled by Western colonial powers, such as Great Britain, France, Germany, Italy and Spain. If we take the case of India, for a very long time, the Britishers had the authority to portray and present the natives of the Indian subcontinent to the rest of the world. Most of these representations in the form of photographs, books, newspapers articles, stories, videos and other media stories portrayed Indians as dark and savage. Dark skin colour in their narratives was used to convey that Indians were primitive. 'Dark skin' was used as a trope to label us as a community incapable of self-governance. The brown-skinned Indian was called the 'white man's burden'. The preference for fair skin is, thus, an enduring legacy of British imperialism. It is, however, crucial to acknowledge that the colonial project was not the only factor reinforcing this pervasive practice of discrimination on the basis of skin colour. Discrimination on the basis of skin colour was a dominant practice within our centuries-old caste system in India. Sunil Bhatia, professor and chair of Human Development at the Connecticut College, explains:

> The term for caste, 'varna', in India's ancient epic the
> Mahabharata refers to colour. With Brahmins—the upper
> caste—being designated as white. The lowest caste—the
> untouchables—are described as dark or black. There is
> a continuing debate in sociology and history about the
> link between skin colour, caste and socio-economic status.
> In modern India, the message is clear: light skin is
> considered superior to dark skin.

This obsession with light skin is reinforced by the processes of globalization and the increased dominance of Western media and narratives in our children's media diet. Let us recall the stories our children read while growing up. From a young age, our children read stories set in countries far away from our realities, representing white people—their culture, lifestyle and habits—and largely written by White writers. For instance, Indian children grow up listening to and reading stories and poems such as 'Snow White', 'Goldilocks and the Three Bears', 'Rapunzel', 'Cinderella' and 'Superman'. In all these stories, the protagonist is a white character. Let us look at one of the most common poems that children are taught in schools in India.

Chubby cheeks, dimpled chin

Rosy lips, teeth within

Curly hair, very fair

Eyes are blue, lovely too.

Teachers pet, is that you?

Yes, Yes, Yes!

When we read this poem critically, we realize that children in India do not have very fair skin or blue eyes. The description in this poem is a prototype of White children in Western countries. If children read such poems from an early age, the 'White child' or the 'White body' becomes their aspirational goal. It is important for children to see people like themselves in the media they consume; when they see their own realities represented in the form of characters who have a similar skin colour, cultural context and language, they feel validated and safe.

In the documentary 'The Illusionists', a British psychotherapist Susie Orbach explains this phenomenon, 'Just as English has become the lingua franca of the world, so the white, blondified, small-nosed, pert-breasted, long-legged body is coming to stand in for the great variety of human bodies that there are.'

How do we challenge this obsession with a white body? How can we develop in our children a sense of appreciation towards a multitude of body types, skin colours, hair textures and facial features? How do we convince them that dark is also beautiful?

There are some steps that we can follow in our families and communities. These include the following:

1. *Using sensitive language:* We cannot stress enough the role of language in shaping how we think and feel about ourselves. The first thing we can do as adults is stop using stereotypes, skin-based slurs and body-related abuses in our families and societies. Emphasize that your child is beautiful, not despite their dark skin colour but because of their skin colour.

2. *Increasing representation:* Ensure that your children's media diet includes stories, shows, books, poems, games, where different body types, skin colour, hair and features are represented with respect. Rely more on local narratives, that is, stories that are contextualized in the Indian context with characters who represent the realities of families and people in India. Include books by writers such as Rabindranath Tagore, Premchand, Jhumpa Lahiri, Salman Rushdie, Ruskin Bond, Sudha Murthy, Anushka Ravishankar and Roopa Pai in your children's reading list.

3. *Disassociate with 'whiteness':* Make active efforts to help children disassociate themselves from their obsession with white skin. Introduce your children to young achievers who are dark, intelligent, sensitive and beautiful. Equip them with information on how discrimination prevails in our societies and how this discrimination limits them. Spend time watching and critiquing popular media, especially commercials, and help them identify stereotypes and prejudices.

4. Do not shy away from accepting and explaining issues related to skin-based discrimination in our societies. Help your children understand how these issues emerged and continue to exist. Introducing them to other parallel movements against the 'white ideal body type' around the world can help them gain a global perspective on the issue. Discussing the global movement 'Black Lives Matter' can be a very effective way of unpacking to your children how race-based or skin colour-based discrimination oppresses, limits and controls us.

5. Every time a family member, relative or any other known person passes a negative remark about someone's skin colour, intervene and explain why these remarks are derogatory, uncritical and discriminatory. This may lead to uncomfortable situations, but if we do not learn to deal with discomfort a few times, we won't be able to change our cultures and societies.

In the next section, we look at the different body types and discuss ways to cultivate a sense of appreciation for these differences.

ACCEPTING DIFFERENCES IN BODY TYPES

Negative Remark	True Compliment
You are very pretty for a fat girl.	You are beautiful.
You are dark but who cares? You are so intelligent.	You are handsome and intelligent.
This dress makes you look thin.	You look wonderful in this dress.
This colour suits you…. You look fair.	I think this colour looks very good on you. It makes your skin glow.
You lost weight. OMG! You look so nice now.	It seems like you have been taking good care of your body. You look fit and healthy.
You have gained weight! Now you won't look like a stick and clothes will suit you.	You look very fit and healthy.

We are built with unique body types, features and characteristics. Body positive movement promotes respect and appreciation for all types of bodies. On Instagram, there are more than 12.8 million posts with the hashtag body positive. Body positivity argues that people should

- have a positive body image and should be able to appreciate their bodies;
- be able to accept and appreciate differences in bodies and respect others;
- help build each other's confidence and acceptance of their own bodies; and
- critique and discard unrealistic body goals.

Body positivity helps people understand how their concept about self, bodies and others is often shaped by social biases, other people's response to our bodies and appearances, and the prevailing beauty standards. Body positivity is a critical task of unpacking how popular media contributes towards the relationship people have with their food, bodies, appearances, identity and self-care. Understanding this relationship will help people identify why and how they develop a negative self and body image. Most importantly, understanding why we think about our bodies and ourselves in a negative light can encourage people to adopt new and more positive ways of engaging with self and others.

Human bodies are different, varied and have flaws. The media-saturated world makes us believe that flaws are a sign of weakness, lack of discipline or ugliness. Many studies have found that exposure to media messages portraying an 'ideal physique' is linked to an increase in body image concerns and eating disorder symptoms. Body positivity helps us focus on all the wonderful things our body can do; everything we can experience because of our bodies. It changes our approach towards our bodies—from looking for faults and limitations, we start looking for strengths and qualities. Some of the steps towards body positivity include the following:

- Set a good example for your children. Starving yourself, following crash diets or continuously cribbing about your body is not helpful.

- Use affirmative language and appreciate your children and their bodies. Use phrases such as 'you are so strong', 'I like your dark skin. It makes you look so regal' or 'I like your hair. They are thick and curly.'
- Normalize the flaws in your body. Tummy rolls, belly fat, stretch marks or cellulite on other parts of the body are normal. Do not feel ashamed of it. If you have stretch marks from your pregnancy, it is a sign of courage and not a flaw.
- Follow body positive influencers on social media.
- Ask your children if they are have confidence in their body. Try to address their concerns. Help them acknowledge their talents and boost their confidence.
- Actively practise complimenting and appreciating people with different body types in everyday conversations at homes and in neighbourhoods.
- Use less filters for your photos on the phone or in your homes.
- Watch movies, shows or songs that challenge the ideal body stereotype.
- Apologize for every time you have called someone fat/thin/ ugly, mocked at people's appearances or clothes, or disabilities, and made your children feel that they are not beautiful enough.

NO ONE SHOULD APOLOGIZE FOR THEIR BODIES

When people live with a sense of shame for their bodies, it influences every dimension of their lives—their education, jobs, interactions, friendships and relationships. For instance, dark-skinned people in India are mocked at or feel threatened because of their skin colour and this mars their confidence. A dark-skinned child who is bullied for their skin colour may refuse to participate in theatre and stage activities, may confine themselves to their rooms, may refuse to socialize and attend gatherings and may find it extremely difficult to make friends.

Parents also attach ideas of shame and dignity onto the bodies of their children. If children use their bodies to engage in experiences deemed unethical by their parents, the adult narrative revolves around how their children have shamed their families. Bodily experiences and experimentation should not be narrativized as 'abominal', 'dirty', 'uncouth' or 'shameful'.

Among young girls and boys, for instance, masturbating is a very normal sexual activity and many cultures stigmatize this. As a result, many boys and girls feel that they have annihilated their bodies every time they masturbate. This shame could lead to issues concerning their mental health and/or sexual relationships.

PERIODS AND THE TABOO CULTURE

Another case in point where we make our young girls feel ashamed of their bodies is when they are menstruating. In many families, girls and women are treated as untouchables—they are not allowed to enter the kitchen, cook or even use common surfaces in the house. They are confined to a corner of the house and receive food in separate plates. Many young girls start associating their periods and their bodies with words such as dirty, impure, unhygienic and unclean. Our societies reinforce these negative stereotypes. For instance, whenever we go to buy sanitary napkins, the shopkeeper wraps it in a newspaper and hides it in a black bag. Sanitary napkins and periods are not something that our young girls should feel scared, ashamed or guilty about. Natural bodily processes are ways for us to experience our world in meaningful ways. Ignoring them with a blanket of shame, regret and humiliation can lead to a low self-esteem and a negative body image.

Developing a positive attitude towards our bodies requires us to focus on all the wonderful things our body can do. For instance, instead of being ashamed of their periods, young girls must develop a sense of appreciation for their bodies' capacity to create a new life. Similarly, queer young people must be encouraged to embrace their uniqueness, their distinct sexual identity and to channel their bodies to experience and navigate through the world.

NURTURING YOUR MIND

We often ignore the 'feeling' part for what we can physically achieve and show. To be truly at peace with our bodies, to nourish and care for them and to identify them as our homes, we must change the way we think about them.

We suggest adopting an inward rather than an outward approach when guiding our children in thinking about their bodies. An outward approach focuses on understanding how our bodies determine our position in the society. This is a comparative approach, where people constantly base their self-worth on other people's approval. The inward approach, on the other hand, encourages us to think about how our body helps us experience the world. Our bodies are sensory powerhouses—we see, hear, feel, taste and navigate our environments through our bodies. Even when they aren't flawless, our bodies allow us to understand, explore and learn. An inward approach draws force from feelings of gratitude and contentment. Let us look at the following activity on practising mindfulness.

REFLECTIVE EXERCISE III

Step 1: For a week, spend 5 minutes every day trying to use all of your functioning senses. Smell your favourite scent, watch the sunrise or sunset, listen to the chirping of crickets, hold a hot glass of milk in your hands during the winters and splash cold water all over your face in the summers.

Step 2: As you are doing this, think about the potential of your body. Appreciate the sensual possibilities that it has to offer.

Step 3: On the last day of this exercise, define what beauty, happiness and pleasure mean to you and how your body helped you enjoy these?

We can practice the following principles to challenge the ideal 'body standards' normalized in our families, communities and societies.

- *Affirmation:* Speak about yourself and others in ways that will build confidence. In times of self-doubt, reach out to people who will affirm your value and worth. Close relatives and friends who are sensitive and positive can be very helpful in enabling us overcome phases of self-doubt and criticism.
- *Intention:* Make efforts every day to look at your body and self with a sense of gratitude, excitement and content. Be aware of the many ways in which your body gives you pleasure and comfort.
- *Action:* Invest time taking care of and appreciating your bodies. Relaxing and enjoying leisure activities are the processes of rejuvenating your bodies and mind. Practise mindfulness and joy in the things you do with your bodies every day. Do not abuse your body with negativity, overindulgence, constant comparison or hatred.

In the next section, we discuss a few exercises and steps to practise self-love in our everyday lives.

Self-love

Remember the instructions we get from airplane safety procedures? Wear your own oxygen mask before helping anyone else.

The same applies to body positive thinking. We must learn to love and appreciate our own body before helping our children or others. Loving and appreciating our body is a life-long process. All of us experience uncertainty, doubt and low esteem about our bodies once in a while. Maybe our skin has suddenly erupted with acne, or we have put on or lost some weight, or we are experiencing hair fall. As we sat down writing this chapter, we realized how some of these insecurities are so deep-rooted that we have to constantly strive to unlearn them and find new ways of loving ourselves and our bodies.

So how do we practise self-love?

Three elements are very important for practising self-love, or any love for that matter: care, appreciation and acceptance.

First is the element of 'care' that manifests itself in the way we support, build and protect the people we love. Second is the element of 'appreciation', which can be witnessed in the ways we express our gratitude for what we love. And the third element is 'acceptance', which emphasizes that the things or people we love can never be perfect, and so we must find ways to deal with limitations and focus on redeeming qualities instead. We can then decide to think of everyday actions through which we can practise care, appreciation and acceptance towards our bodies.

Care

Care is practised in ways that are meant to enhance and further the well-being and potential of our bodies and minds. If our lifestyle or dietary habits place our bodies and minds in the 'inactive', 'lethargic' and 'sad' zones, we must re-examine our routines and change them accordingly. When we practise care in our routines, our children learn from observing our behaviour. Some steps towards caring for our bodies and minds can include the following:

1. Right from a young age, make sure that children eat home-cooked, healthy food full of greens and fruits. Some parents encourage their children to eat from the 'canteen' because they do not have enough time to prepare food at home. Doing this on a regular basis leads to unhealthy eating and disrespect towards our bodies. One solution is to involve the entire family in food preparation. Children should be able to prepare simple lunches for themselves once they are pre-teens or teens. Providing a healthy diet for the family should not be the mother's responsibility alone. Also, parents can ration the intake of 'junk/unhealthy' food for their children to once or twice a week. This will, however, require that parents follow the same regime and eat at home.

2. Exercise with your family. Go for walks, practise yoga or do other physical activities, such as playing a sport, dancing or hiking. Plan active weekends and vacations instead of spending those days in front of the screen. Encourage children to step away from the 'screens' and explore the outdoors. Visits to parks, zoos, gyms and yoga studios can be an interesting way of spending quality time together. Even the occasional home cleaning sessions could be scheduled for family time. Inculcate pride in doing home chores and keeping the surroundings tidy. With an increase in the spread of media and the Internet, many children find themselves glued to their screens—playing video games or watching shows and cartoons. Parents also have the same habits of leisure and relaxation that makes for an extremely sedentary lifestyle and can cause health issues. It is important to include 30 minutes of physical workout in our routines.

The other day we were visiting a colleague. She has two teenage, college going children. The entire time we were there, we were surprised at how the children constantly asked the household help for everything—a glass of water, a spoon, to open the door, to find a misplaced car key! The parents didn't find anything wrong in this, but observing this made us wonder what kind of adults these children would grow into?

3. Ask your children about their mental health. In India, mental health is still considered to be a taboo subject. If people say they are suffering from mental health problems, they are either termed as *sanki, rotlu, pagal* or dismissed as weak, emotional or *dramebaaz*. To overcome this stigma attached with discussion around mental health, make sure you constantly ask your family members about their mental well-being. Also, in some cases of mental health crisis, family members or relatives are incompetent to help. In such situations, parents shouldn't fear taking help of counsellors and mental health experts. Normalize that mental health sometimes deteriorates and weakens just like our physical health. Normalize that people can experience emotions and feelings they do not know how to deal with. Normalize that seeking help, reaching out and expressing vulnerability are very important for the well-being of both individuals and their families.

Appreciation

Expressing gratitude for your body and mind, appreciating how our bodies and minds help us achieve so many daily goals and how they enable us to experience the world is the starting step towards loving ourselves. Many health coaches and psychologists suggest a 40-day 'mirror challenge'. According to this challenge, people are encouraged to look at themselves in the mirror every day for 40 days and to thank their bodies and minds for the things they were able to do during the day. We practised this challenge with a few of our friends and family members. One of the participants said:

> I have acne on my face, and I am so conscious about it. The minute I step out of the house, I feel people are staring at my face. Nobody even notices my acne until I bring it up myself, which I often do. When I did the mirror challenge for 40 days, I felt a little differently about my acne problem. I am still conscious but now I have learnt how to distract myself and focus on other things my body can do. I am more confident while talking to people now; I can look them in the eyes, whereas earlier I used to try and cast my eyes away from them so that I wouldn't be watching them looking at my face.

Another exercise for appreciating our bodies involves practising mindfulness. Being mindful of our body, the way it functions and the pleasure and possibilities it grants us helps with developing a sense of gratitude for what we have. Let us look at the following one-minute exercises for practising mindfulness towards our body.

ONE-MINUTE WELL-BEING EXERCISES

1. *Stretch for 10 seconds every hour:* Every hour, take a 10-second break to stretch and to feel your body. Stretching will reorient us towards our bodies and how we feel in them.
2. *Stroke your hands:* Close your eyes and feel your hands rubbing against each other.
3. *Mindfully eat a raisin or any other treat:* Sense the treat you are eating—how it smells, feels, tastes, its texture and consistency. Translate this practice to eating your food mindfully. Most importantly, enjoy your food.

4. *Pray to your body*: Twice every day, close your eyes and say this prayer: May I be healthy, may I be peaceful, may I love my body.

5. *Mindful breathing*: Every day, pause for a minute and count the number of breaths you draw.

Practising appreciation helps unhook our self-worth from our appearance and reorients us towards developing a holistic understanding of the role of mind and body in our lives. It is critical to delink our self-image from how we assume people perceive our bodies. Our bodies are meant to be more than just a 'cover' and 'appearance'. Appreciate your bodies as a means through which we understand what it means to be alive and living and consider it a blessing.

Acceptance

Appreciating our bodies also includes being aware of how they are constituted—traits, features, characteristics and limitations. Some bodies are thin and lean, while others are broad and strong. Some people have more melanin in their skin while others don't. Appreciating how we are designed differently and how our body is unique is crucial towards identifying its limitations and weaknesses. We can always find a few good traits in our body. Many young girls, for instance, fall prey to the ideal body narrative and experience low self-esteem if their breasts are not big and visible. Many girls who have smaller breasts are called ' flat tires', 'planks,' 'blackboard' and other derogatory names in their schools and neighbourhoods. On the contrary, girls who develop breasts earlier than their peers are also made to feel self-conscious and called names. The first step towards challenging the 'ideal body type' is to accept that different women have different kinds of breasts and healthy breasts come in varying sizes and shapes. Height, body type, skin colour, hair, features, are all genetic endowments, and no amount of work can alter them drastically. Accepting our body, the way it is designed and structured, allows us to re-evaluate our expectations and bodily aspirations. Of course, we are free to experiment with style, accessories and make-up if they help us feel more confident. The important thing is that these external props should not be harmful, painful or draining on our pockets, and we should not crave for them just to look acceptable in the eyes of the others.

You may not control all the events that happen to you, but you can decide not to be reduced by them.

—Maya Angelou in her book
Letter to My Daughter

Caring for, appreciating and accepting our bodies and minds will help us look at our lives in meaningful ways. It is important to remember that radical self-love helps us to embrace #everybodyasabeachbody, to make consistent efforts to maintain and further the well-being of our bodies and minds, and to seek help when needed.

In this chapter, we have only focused on how the media and our social prejudices join hands in discriminating against people on the basis of their skin colour and body shapes. Similar discrimination also happens when the media constantly portrays certain communities, classes, religions or castes in a stereotypical way. Again, we have two weapons against this: produce and consume more sensitive media and challenge such discrimination in our families, schools and communities.

CHAPTER 7

Using Technology to Connect and Learn

CHILDHOOD: ONLINE AND OFFLINE

These days, as parents and teachers, we have a love–hate relationship with technology. We are excited at the opportunities and efficiency it brings, hopeful about the bright future it might create for our children, suspicious about what it is stealing from us and downright fearful about it snatching away our children from us. Well, love it or hate it, technology is here to stay and, therefore, making friends with the monster is to our best advantage.

Tick all the boxes which apply to your children and their routines

- ❏ Owns a personal mobile phone, laptop or any other electronic device
- ❏ Is constantly in touch with friends
- ❏ Membership on Netflix, Amazon Prime, Disney or other online streaming channels
- ❏ Profiles on social media such as Facebook, Twitter, Instagram or Pinterest
- ❏ WhatsApp on the phone
- ❏ Takes a lot of selfies and shares photos with others—publicly or privately
- ❏ Refuses to share their mobile phones or personal devices with other members of the family
- ❏ Loves spending time playing games online
- ❏ Has online friends, that is, people children meet and befriend online
- ❏ Uses their laptops and other devices for homework and education
- ❏ Refuses to leave their phones at home while going for outings
- ❏ Brings their devices to the dining table
- ❏ Thinks parents are too naive to understand why they are so attached to their phones and other devices

In our interactions with parents across the country, we have come across several instances where parents have expressed discomfort with their children being glued to their phones. Many parents complain that their children spend less time with them, do not enjoy face-to-face conversations with them or with guests anymore and are easily distracted by their phones, laptops and other devices. This fear of technology, especially mobile phones, taking over our lives is particularly relevant in many middle-class, urban families in India.

This fear related to children's use of technology, especially mobile phones and laptops, emerges from a sense of anxiety about the penetration and all-pervasive role of technologies, the Internet and electronic devices in our homes and families. There is no denying that these technological devices are changing our lives and societies, but this change is inevitable, and so it is critical that we learn how to embrace this new reality of blurring boundaries between online and offline; the reel and the real.

Our children who have access to the Internet and technological devices spend a lot of time online. Even from within the confines of their rooms and homes, they relate to ideas, people and phenomena spanning across geographical boundaries and limits. This is both good and bad. Let us look at the following scenarios.

> *Scene A:* Sohail is a 13-year-old boy from New Delhi who uses his laptop and mobile phone for educational purposes as well as to connect with his friends and peers. He spends a lot of time online, even when he is doing his homework. His parents are worried that he will not be able to perform well academically if he continues being distracted by his phones and the constant online chatter.
>
> *Scene B:* Rishika is a 14-year-old girl from Ahmedabad, and her parents refuse to allow their daughter to use mobile phones at all. The family has a landline connection, and Rishika's friends are expected to contact her on that

number. Her parents have their personal cell phones, but they do not use them in front of Rishika. Rishika often complains that she misses out on a lot of fun and interactions among her classmates on WhatsApp groups because she doesn't have a phone.

Scene C: Amyra is a 12-year-old girl from Mumbai who has unrestricted access to technological devices and the Internet. She owns a personal phone, has a video game console in her bedroom and has profiles on Facebook and Instagram. Her parents believe in allowing their child to practise autonomy in how she wants to use the Internet and her technological devices.

If we analyse these situations closely, we will realize that mobile phones and the Internet are indispensable features of urban childhood in India. The question is: how do we make sense of our anxieties while encouraging our children to optimize their use of technology for personal growth and development? How can we embrace technology with an intention of expanding the learning, educational and communication horizons of our children? How can we think about childhood and adolescence in relation to the undeniable presence of technology and the Internet? In short, how do we increase their opportunities and minimize their risks?

THE NEW CHILDHOOD

Childhood is now a phase in the lives of our children that lies at the intersection of online and offline experiences. The boundaries between our living realities and the virtual world are gradually blurring or becoming invisible. Children are surrounded by technologies in their homes, schools and communities, and, by that logic, they are always connected to people, ideas and events beyond their immediate reach. Constant exposure to unrestricted information and connections influences our children's experiences in three significant ways:

1. Children are spending more time developing and nurturing relationships and connections virtually or with their technologies, and this can have some influence on their ability to hold and engage in face-to-face communication. Sherry Turkle,[1] a leading psychologist at MIT, emphasizes that face-to-face conversations during childhood are crucial for children to develop empathy and sensitivity towards their families, communities and societies. If a balance is not maintained, face-to-face conversations will be eclipsed by virtual connections, and children will find it difficult to learn and interpret social cues, emotions and gestures that are integral to the conversational nature of human societies. Turkle argues that technologies create an illusion of caring machines and that children can be extremely vulnerable to this technological allure.

> Can you imagine what would happen if a child is constantly interacting with technological/voice-based assistants such as Alexa and Siri? They would assume that a normal pattern of interaction is that they ask, and the others answer, they command and the others obey. Such children would find it difficult to deal with human interaction where they would be questioned, challenged or ignored. Spending considerably long amounts of time with technological devices and away from real, offline social interactions may not only hinder the development of relational skills among children but may also encourage them to make negative progress. Turkle[2] explains:

---

[1] S. Turkle, *Reclaiming Conversation: The Power of Talk in a Digital Age* (New York, NY: Penguin Publishing House, 2015).

[2] W. Parry, 'Is Your Kid Friends with Alexa? A Psychologist on What That Means for Their Development', NBC News (2018). Available at https://www.nbcnews.com/mach/science/your-kid-friends-alexa-psychologist-what-means-their-development-ncna896576 (accessed on 23 November 2020).

A machine always has a response ready. You never have to wait, to attend to silences or to what one young woman I interviewed called the 'boring bits' in conversation. We can forget the kind of listening and the kind of talking about our feelings that real conversation requires.

2. Childhood is no more limited to what can be accessed or experienced physically. This includes the overflow of information and access to multiple sources of entertainment and education available at a click of the button. Indiscriminately using this information can overwhelm children and their parents, but a judicious use can allow them to expand their horizons of knowledge and communication. The risks in online encounters are real, but there are also opportunities to grow and become a better human being. For instance, the time children spend on the Internet can either be used to introduce them to different realities in the world, connect them with people from different cultures and regions, albeit in safe ways, or it may lead them to create echo-chambers and replicate their offline networks in their online worlds.

3. Virtual connections and digital networks can redefine offline realities for many children, as it may grant them access to skills, opportunities and learning experiences that might otherwise have been inaccessible to them. This can produce significant changes in their lives, giving them better career opportunities, networking possibilities and guidance or mentorship in the form of virtual connections. For instance, many organizations conduct online contests, conferences and workshops inviting children from across the country and around the globe to participate in meaningful experiences. Also, the Internet enables a low capital-intensive environment where children can learn to use digital tools and techniques to create, play with and implement novel ideas related to issues of their

interest. For instance, many young people in India appreciate Japanese anime, K-pop and BTS, and are actively involved in online social activism and justice.

Technologies, especially smartphones that foster connection and exchanges anytime anywhere, have become an inevitable part of children's everyday lives. In the following section, we draw special attention to the role of the Internet and digital networks in the everyday lives of children in India.

THE INTERNET AND THE EVERYDAY LIFE

LET US PAUSE AND THINK!

Take five minutes to chart your children's routines—what they do from the time they wake up to the time they go to bed. Pay special attention to how and when your children use the Internet—in smartphones, TVs, laptops, Kindles, Tablets and other devices.

To monitor the daily media habits of your children, you can record the time they spend doing activities related to media consumption. Your children use media for entertainment, education, connection or some other purposes. You can note down the time your children spend doing various media-related activities. It would be interesting to do this by yourself first and later compare your observations with what your children have to say about their Internet use! How accurate is your perception? After you have created this list for your children, repeat the same process to document your own Internet use daily. As an additional fun and perhaps eye-opening step, you can ask your children to chart your Internet use too.

This activity in self-analysis will reveal that, on an average, we spend most of our days on our devices using the Internet for work, entertainment, leisure or connectivity. The Internet defines all aspects of the lives of our children, more so after the pandemic. In March 2020, when the entire world was dealing with the COVID-19 pandemic, most countries announced a lockdown and children were confined to their homes. Every aspect of our offline lives went online—schools, work, shopping, entertainment, family gatherings, game nights and conversations. Although the effects of the pandemic are brought under control and the world is opening up, the COVID-19 lockdown is a glance into our future societies, where the Internet will be the most significant mediating platform for connection and communication across regions and ideologies.

Have we given enough attention to how our children will be raised in a world that is increasingly defined by the Internet, virtual communities and digital networks? Can we create a home environment that is conducive to such a technologized possibility? Or are we scared that such a world, replete with unimaginable possibilities, will destroy human societies and relations?

The proliferation of the Internet and digital networks have rendered the entire globe accessible to children with smartphones and Internet connections. Let us consider the flow of media products from different countries of the world to India through various online streaming platforms such as Netflix, Prime, Hulu, Disney and others. Here, the circulation of media products also entails exposure to different cultures, societies and realities represented through those narratives. For instance, many young children in India are familiar with Japanese culture because they regularly consume anime. These children are often part of online anime fan communities consisting of members from across the world, belonging to different regions, religions, societies and speaking different languages. Children develop meaningful relationships through such interactions and cultivate ideas about themselves—who they are, where they belong and what their priorities in life are. Yes, if we are controlling parents and think that our culture and religion are the best with no flaws and that exposing children to different ideas would undermine our control, we will look at this reality with fear and suspicion. Unfortunately, there is no way of controlling this reality, but there are ways to face it wisely and meaningfully.

In the following section, we will explore how children's engagement through and with the Internet influences their identity and understanding of the world.

CHILDREN AS CITIZENS OF THE WORLD

Do you agree that we live in a connected world? Let us think through this together. Many schools in India follow an international board curriculum and introduce children to the ideas of global citizenship from a young age. Each year, many students from India travel to different countries in the world for education, travel, employment and so on. Similarly, many multinational corporations in India recruit employees from different countries, and their presence creates a multicultural environment in our cities and towns. Various universities hold international conferences, workshops and summer schools to encourage students from different countries to develop global empathy and sensitivity as they grow up in a highly connected world. As families, Indians have been traveling more and more globally, and global brands are seen everywhere in urban India. Given the increasing importance of global and international relations and communications in our lives, we must encourage our children to develop knowledge and interpersonal skills that are critical to navigate through globalized and technologized societies.

Countries have realized that our digitally connected world sustains interdependence and mutual respect for differences. As parents and teachers, it is our responsibility to nurture children as citizens of the world who are not fearful or anxious of differences but meet them with curiosity and interest. Digital platforms and networks, our social media platforms and the Internet have all afforded us innumerable opportunities to help our children experience the multicultural fabric of the world from their homes and schools.

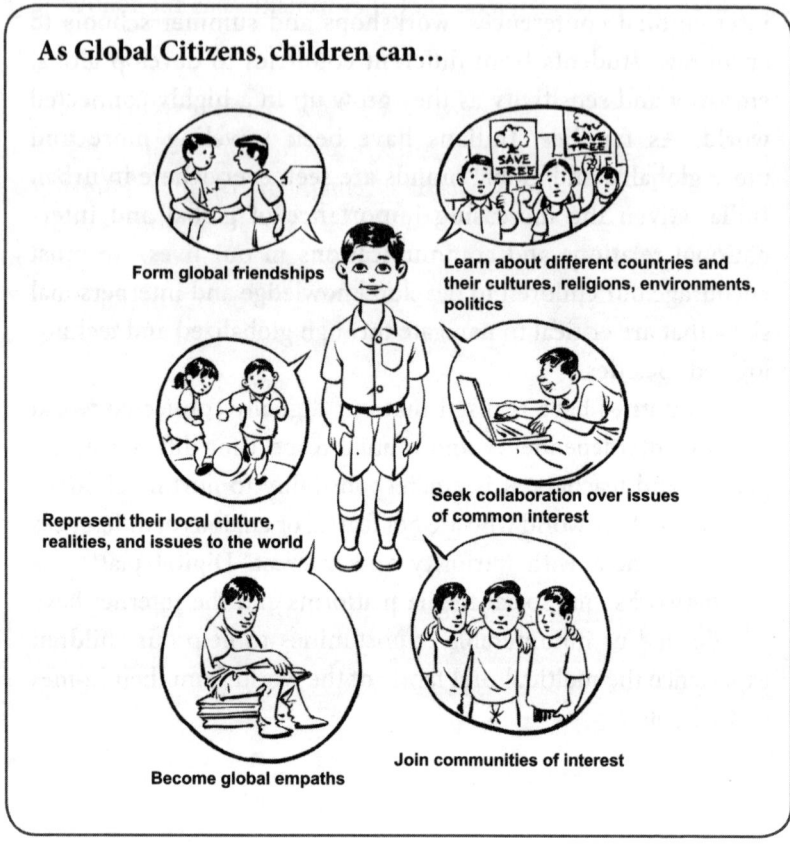

As Global Citizens, children can...

Form global friendships

Learn about different countries and
their cultures, religions, environments,
politics

Represent their local culture,
realities, and issues to the world

Seek collaboration over issues
of common interest

Become global empaths

Join communities of interest

Before we can introduce our children to the idea of 'citizens of the
world', we must first define what it means to be a global citizen.
First, being a global citizen does not mean that we stop being
the citizen of our country or lose all attachment to our city, state
and local culture. We can be local, national and global citizens
at the same time. Being a global citizen means more than just
eating global food, watching and listening to global media and
using global brands. At the heart of global citizenship is the concept
of shared human experience, which transcends geographical,

cultural and other barriers. Global citizenship has the following distinct features.

- *Transcultural awareness:* We have been exploring the concept of transcultural citizenship for some time now. In her work, *Global Civic Engagement on Online Platforms: Women as Transcultural Citizens*, Shelat[3] introduced the concept of 'transcultural' awareness to argue that though people are now globally connected through the Internet and digital networks, they are still rooted in their local realities. Transcultural awareness is a very critical feature of globally oriented children and emphasizes that young people experience the world—different people, regions, countries and communities—culturally and relationally. For instance, students who participate in global exchange programmes develop close bonds with individuals from other countries and learn about different cultures and communities in and through their interpersonal interactions with their global partners. At the same time, students who have never travelled abroad due to lack of resources can also forge such ties and friendships through online communities or even through reading books from across the world. Books are the cheapest way to get a glimpse of the world.

  Shelat also emphasizes the importance of the local in today's globalized world, and that is the second component of global citizenship.

- *Rootedness in local realities:* Globally oriented people operate from within their local, everyday realities. For instance, when a young person from India writes blogs on social issues related

---

[3] M. Shelat, *Global Civic Engagement on Online Platforms: Women as Transcultural Citizens* (Madison, WI: University of Wisconsin-Madison, 2016).

to the environment or gender equality for international and global platforms, they will provide examples and instances on the basis of what they observe in their cities and communities. At the same time, our local realities are changing every day because of global influences. For instance, the uproar around Black Lives Matter in May 2020 in international media encouraged many people in India to question colourism and caste-based discrimination in their own societies. As a result of this, young people in India compelled Fair and Lovely to rebrand itself and challenged the practice of colourism. Although this is a very small step, it exemplifies how global issues influence our local experiences. To be globally oriented, young people must relate to their local communities and then form links globally. If this does not happen, they might feel rootless and lost.

- *Technological and safety skills:* The Internet and digital networks can help us to develop a multicultural perspective. We understand and learn to respect different cultures. This certainly does not mean that all people everywhere are the same. The Internet allows children to experience the world and the differences inherent in human societies first-hand. How else can you do this at such a low cost without travelling abroad? If we equip our children or rather support them to equip themselves with the necessary technological skills and safety measures, children can use online spaces as learning spaces. It helps them to reach places and people beyond their physical reach, to meet people with very different ideologies and to learn how to engage with these differences.
- *Adaptability:* The rate of change these days is so rapid that all of us have to learn to accept and adapt to change. Everything around us and our children is changing dramatically—from modes of teaching and learning to ways of communicating and connecting to systems of trade and commerce to jobs and ways to meet possible suitors.

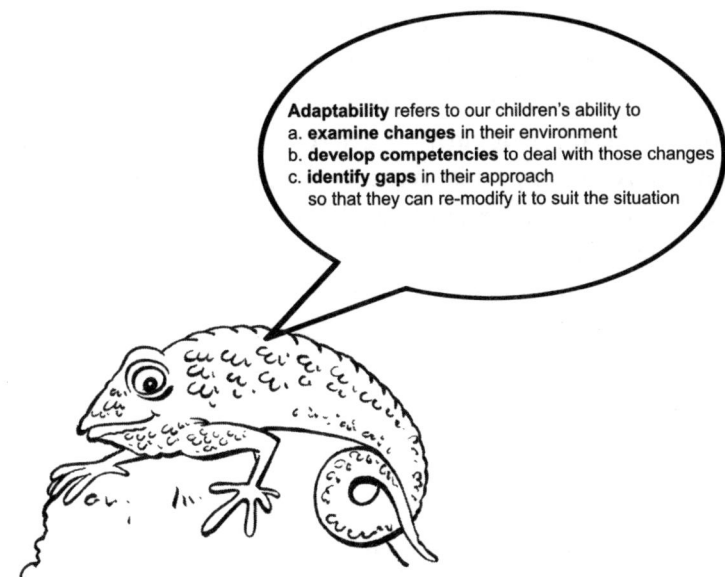

Adaptability refers to our children's ability to
a. **examine changes** in their environment
b. **develop competencies** to deal with those changes
c. **identify gaps** in their approach
   so that they can re-modify it to suit the situation

In India, many parents are at a loss of words when their tech-savvy children throw technological and Internet-based jargons at them. For instance, let us understand the experience of a mother with two teenage children who are constantly glued to their phones and laptops.

As soon as my children got their personal phones and study laptops, they started talking in a totally different language. When I say language, I also mean that their lifestyle changed, and I could not connect with them anymore. They stopped watching TV with us (parents) in the living room. They spent more time in their bedrooms talking to their friends on video calls.

I remember, I was calling out for my daughter to come join us for dinner one day when she texted me from her room, which is literally 10 steps away from the dining area, and told me that she is going to bed. She finished her text with 'ttyl'.

I lost my cool. I had spent so much effort cooking that dinner for them and they could not step out of their rooms and away from their phones to tell me that they are not hungry. In the spur of the moment, I got very angry with her but, on further reflection, I realized two things. Mobile phones are changing our understanding about privacy and intimacy. They are also changing the way we talk—words, sentences, emotions, gestures that we use through our phones. If I have to keep up with this changing generation, I cannot shy away from technology. I may not be a 'pro' at it like these kids who have grown up with technology, but I can learn to use these devices to my advantage.

When parents refuse to learn how to use the Internet and other new technologies, they create a 'generational distance' between themselves and their tech-savvy children. This distance generally manifests itself in ways such as children overriding parental authority in issues related to technology use such as the time they should spend with their gadgets, things they should do online and people they should befriend. As parents and educators, it is important we keep abreast with technological advancements, learn how to use the Internet and social media to help children become more sensitive and socially aware individuals and guide them away from dangerous terrains such as cyberbullying, identity thefts, fake information and online hatred. It is not necessary to learn every new app and be an expert gamer. Of course, as adults, we have other priorities and interests. It helps, however, to know the basics so that we can engage in conversations with our children and don't always see their internet use with suspicion and resentment. In what follows, we describe ways in which parents can become tech-savvy and help their children conquer the realm of the Internet and social media platforms.

BECOMING A TECH-SAVVY PARENT

FROM THE DIARY OF A 40-YEAR-OLD MOTHER IN DELHI

Back in our days, we did not have all these gadgets. My younger son is 13 years old, and he is always on his phone, or laptop and so on. I have often found my younger son struggling with things on the Internet—sometimes he does not know how to browse more effectively, which links to follow and so on. My older son helps him, but you know how it is among siblings—if they are fighting, they will never help each other.

After lockdown was declared in Delhi due to the spread of COVID-19, I received an e-mail from my children's school announcing that they will be conducting the remaining classes online. This means that it was the parents' responsibility to ensure that their children were attentive during these online sessions. Now, my younger son is very smart and can easily fool me, and he thinks his mother does not understand technology, so he spent all his time browsing his Facebook for the first week of these online classes. My elder son saw this and brought it to my notice. I felt bad. I was sitting right next to my younger son, and I could not understand what he was doing. I am a working woman and with this 'work-from-home' arrangement, I am also learning how to use my laptop efficiently. So I decided to learn how to block these sites on my laptop and added some parental locks on my son's laptop for the duration of his online classes.

If we do not learn how to use these gadgets, our children will take us for a ride and when they do that, we will not be able to educate, protect and guard them against potential threats and dangers online.

THE STRANGER DANGER

Now, here is a serious parenting dilemma. Should we allow our children to connect with communities and people we do not know in the offline world, or we insist that they use the Internet and social media to connect only with people we are familiar with. If we choose the first option, there is a good possibility that we and our children will use the Internet and social media to create a new and safe public space where people can think through ideas, concepts and strategies to further their political, personal and social aspirations. At the same time, the Internet is full of harmful people too—paedophiles, sexual abusers, scamsters, extremists and bullies. If we use the Internet only to remain in touch with people we already know, we are, however, not making the best use of its potential.

Before we plunge into this discussion, let us examine the role of the Internet and social media platforms in initiating and sustaining discussions, deliberations, activism and creating supportive communities.

Many scholars refer to the Internet and social media as virtual public spaces where large-scale networks can be forged and young people can learn critical conversational skills. These are great places to develop what we call a 'public voice'. Children use their social media profiles to create an identity that they want to project for themselves. They use their profiles and networks to communicate who they are, what they believe in and who they wish to connect with. The simple act of posting, responding to other people's posts, sharing information, discussing and creating new content to argue and present their opinions, ideas or stories can enable them to practise autonomy. Virtual communities also provide nurturing spaces for those children who do not find adequate support in their local communities. For instance, it may be difficult for a gay child in India to find support groups and networks within their own immediate local communities. In such cases, virtual support groups, friendships and mentorship over social media platforms and the Internet can prove to be very effective in helping children make sense of their feelings, emotions, mental conflicts and other issues. Similarly, many young people resort to the Internet to read, study and understand practices of 'safe sex' because their family members do not feel comfortable talking about sexual health with them.

LET US LOOK AT SOME OTHER SIMILAR CASES

1. Shreenita is a 16-year-old girl who lives in Mumbai. She loves art and craft, and wants to dedicate more time learning how to paint. Both her parents have a 9-to-5 job schedule and do not have the time or energy to pick and drop her to an art and craft class after school. Shreenita decided to join the Fun Crafts Kid Facebook group, where she attends free live sessions with arts and crafts instructors who teach young people different skills regularly. She has also made friends with other members from the USA, Spain and Singapore. They have created a five-member group online and they share their arts and crafts items with each other regularly.

2. Rakesh, a 15-year-old boy from Mumbai, is a member of an international WhatsApp cooking group, where the group admin, a famous cook, posts recipes of different cuisines and encourages members from different countries to experiment with them and send their feedback. He has learned how to bake, grill and make gourmet dishes from this online group, free of cost.

3. Miss Bernie is a high school teacher in Ahmedabad, and she has created a WhatsApp group where she posts sample

question papers, quiz exams and interesting resources to help her students. Using WhatsApp allows Miss Bernie to interact with her students and discuss educational topics even after class hours.

In all these cases, children, teachers and parents use the Internet to surpass geographical or other practical barriers to learning, communicating and networking. Such communities are usually productive and should also take extra care in ensuring that our children learn how to use the Internet safely. Can we think of ways in which children can use the Internet to connect beyond classrooms, local and national borders, and learn to embrace differences?

CONNECTING BEYOND BORDERS AND DIFFERENCES

The authors conducted a study in which they interviewed 20 young bloggers from around the world to understand how they were using online global spaces such as Voices of Youth (managed by UNICEF) and Youthink (managed by the World Bank) and websites such as TakingITGlobal, Global Voices and Youth Ki Awaaz to blog about global, social, political, cultural and economic issues. Three things were evident from these interviews.

1. Young people from around the world have similar civic interests and want to collaborate with others to think about ways to change the world. For instance, many young bloggers from different countries connected over the issue of environmental conservation. They discussed ways in which they could protect their environment and write/sign petitions demanding the governments and corporations to adopt more environment-friendly policies. Although these children had different lifestyles, experiences, cultures and societies, the

Internet allowed them to identify points of similarity with others and bridge the existing differences through collective teamwork. The Internet networks and platforms help young people to find common connections with others and use those similarities to bridge cultural gaps.

2. To forge global connections, young people need adult guidance and encouragement. In a report from the study Global Kids Online, scholars argued that very few children use the Internet on their own for creative purposes. Many are not aware of such opportunities and it is therefore the responsibility of parents and educators to introduce children to creative, communicative and global possibilities over the Internet. Instead of spending endless hours on Facebook scrolling through other people's feeds, children can be encouraged to use their timeline to blog about issues that are of interest to them. The infrastructure of social media and the Internet is revolutionary because it enables connections, creations and networking across countries and platforms at affordable rates. Also, the Internet offers rich resources in mentorship, guidance or training. YouTube has many tutorials on several topics: from gardening, cooking, solving math problems, coding, dancing to artwork, public speaking, rhetoric and much more. Some of these platforms can also open possibilities for spending quality parent–child time.

3. Engaging with others over creative pursuits or issues of civic importance can help our children identify ways in which they can understand themselves and the world better. For instance, young people from India discussing feminism and gender equality with others in the Arab countries may realize that people's lived realities influence their understanding of feminism. For a woman who has been raised in an extremely conservative and patriarchal society, arguing with her parents to allow her to complete her education is an act of challenging gender inequality. On the other hand, for a girl who belongs to

a very progressive and feminist family, the right to education may not even be an issue of conflict or discussion. The process of developing sensitivity and empathy for other people, and being considerate of their life struggles and realities, is called 'intersectional' understanding.

Emphasis on going global in no way means that we are suggesting a distance from the local. In the following section, we discuss how our global connections and understanding must be intrinsically tied to our local realities.

UNDERSTANDING YOUR PLACE IN THE WORLD: FROM LOCAL TO GLOBAL

The local is the centrepiece around which young people construct their global participation online. Let us look at the following example.

Scene I

Minakshi is a 16-year-old girl who lives in Delhi. She is enrolled in a school with students belonging to the middle-class background. In school, many students 'slut shame' students on the basis of clothes they wear, people they hang out with or the boys they date. Minakshi has experienced this misogynistic behaviour herself. She was slut-shamed for wearing a tube top to a party at her friend's house.

When Minakshi discusses feminism and gender equality, she focuses primarily on how 'women and girls are not allowed to wear what they want'. She emphasizes, 'Girls should wear what they want.'

Scene II

Dina is a 16-year-old Muslim girl from Washington DC. She knows Minakshi through a Facebook group where young girls discuss feminism, gender equality, girls in stem (science, technology, engineering and maths) and other related issues. When Minakshi shared her experience related to clothing restrictions imposed on girls in her society, Dina shared a similar and yet a very different experience. According to Dina, many of her friends and classmates often make her feel bad about wearing a 'hijab' to classes and gatherings. Her school authorities had once also thought of mandating a 'no hijab in schools' guideline. She is very offended that people continue to dictate how girls should dress or what clothes they should wear.

As is evident in both cases, even while discussing issues of global importance such as feminism, gender equality and women safety, people choose to draw from their localities, their lived experiences and their cultural realities to engage with these issues. Through global connections and communication, these young people develop ways to communicate their local experiences in ways that are relatable to a global audience.

This process, in which young people demonstrate awareness about the world while making sense of and articulating their local realities, is called 'living glocally'. The most powerful case in point are examples of child climate activists from India who are collaborating with child activists from other countries to compel their respective governments to pass the climate change law. Licypriya Kangujam, an eight-year-old climate activist from India, discusses issues related to climate change and conservation drawing from her local experiences of living in India. In her blogs, conversations and online speeches, she discusses the local realities of climate degradation and ties it neatly with the global issue of climate change and global warming. Child activists like her are using local issues to draw attention to a global cause and highlight how many of these societal issues may manifest themselves in different forms locally but will influence the entire world in these highly connected and globalized times.

USING SOCIAL MEDIA PURPOSIVELY

Young people should certainly have the freedom to use social media for fun, leisure, friendship and entertainment, but they can extend their social media use to include practices that allow them to make civic contributions through discussions, online activism and conversations. Such a choice should not be forced on young people, but we should at least introduce them to such possibilities.

Let us first understand what it means for young people to be civically active.

A person with a civic mind has three core characteristics:

1. They try to identify and examine problems in the communities.
2. They try to take responsibility for their actions in relation to society. Some exemplary questions may include: am I littering the streets? Am I encouraging bullying or any form of harassment in my classrooms and playgrounds? Am I not being fair to someone because of my bias?
3. They try to make their communities better through discussions, activism or volunteering.

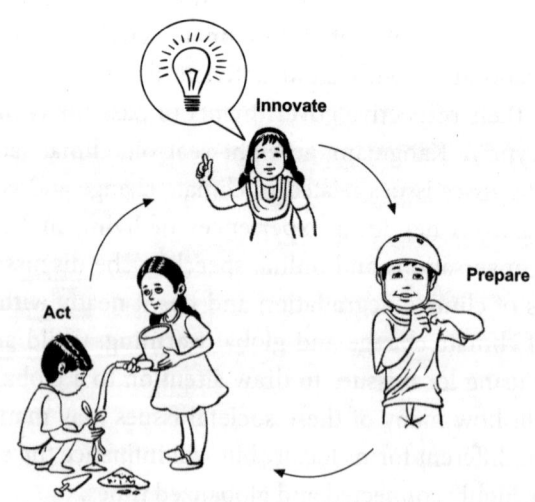

According to UNESCO, social media can provide many opportunities for young people to practise their civic responsibility in
varied contexts (geopolitical, social, historical), forms (advocacy,
information sharing, content creation, mobilization) and community engagements (online community participation, building
and experiencing solidarity, translating online engagement into an
offline collaboration, international/global exchanges).

If our children want to make meaningful connections over
the Internet, it is important that we educate them to use their social
media to create sensitive and well-meaning dialogues with others.

Many scholars in the field of youth studies suggest that young
people sometimes use anonymity and distance embedded in
social media to abuse, bully and threaten others. We must look
at our social media as the new public space where people should
be encouraged to hold civil deliberations and conversations.
Social media can help us to build public conscience if we learn to
harness its power to initiate and sustain civic dialogues on issues
concerning our societies and the world.

ECHO CHAMBERS ON SOCIAL MEDIA

Here, a critical point to consider is how the network algorithms
of social media platforms limit us within echo-chambers.
Algorithmic studies suggest that interactions of individuals on
their social media are determined by their peer networks, that
is, who their friends are, what kinds of posts do they like and
share, who they engage with on a regular basis through their social
media platforms and so on. Young people need critical adult
guidance on how to hold meaningful one-to-one conversations
online with those who lie outside our echo-chambers, that
is, those who have different opinions and ideologies. In the
absence of such guidance, young individuals may continue to
judge, stereotype and bully others. This can reinforce negative
stereotypes and biases about the other. Parents and educators
can guide young people out of their echo-chambers and

help them build inclusive and truly global social media networks and associations. In the following section, we suggest some online strategies that our children might want to use on their social media spaces to generate meaningful dialogues around critical civic issues.

ONLINE STRATEGIES TO BUILD GLOBAL– CIVIC COMMUNITIES

Strategy I. Developing Online Production Skills

Social media platforms can be used to produce and circulate multimedia content to promote specific civic issues. Social media today uses text, videos, images, animation as well as sound. If we must encourage our children to use social media to develop their creative and production skills, we should first familiarize ourselves with the basic content creation principles of each platform.

Twitter content is known for its brevity and precision. It is similar to precis writing skills. The aim is to create short and impactful passages discussing a particular issue.

Instagram is a photo sharing platform that exploits the potential of the visual. To use Instagram effectively, young people must learn how to micro-blog using photos. Photos become the centrepiece around which the narrative is created.

Facebook relies more on interactions between people in the form of comments, responses and messages shared related to any given post. Young people can be encouraged to follow pages such as Voices of Youth, Youth Ki Awaaz, Amy Poehler's Smart Girls and others where young people are encouraged to express their opinions on important civic issues.

YouTube is a wonderful resource for budding and young technologists and artists who wish to share their content with people. Children who want to invite constructive criticism on their talents and work can submit their videos to various online channels for publication.

There are easy and free apps and software available to assist us with the production process.

Strategy II. Apply for Online Youth Development Programmes

When creating content for online audiences, it is important to understand the demands and needs of online communities. For instance, according to many content creators, online videos should not be longer than 1 minute because viewers start losing interest. Videos should also have a compelling storyline. This implies that young people require guidance and mentorship. Many organizations working with youth provide this kind of training. For instance, Voices of Youth and Youth Ki Awaaz have fellowship training programmes where young people are encouraged to collaborate with global partners and co-create blog posts. These blog posts are then edited by senior bloggers to help children understand how they should address the needs of their global online audience. Taking IT Global have volunteering opportunities where children can learn many skills. Some other platforms providing such guidance and training include the UN Youth Climate Summit Blogger Fellowship, the Blogging Program of Development in Action, the World Youth Alliance Blog, ED Times Youth Blog and several others.

Strategy III. Develop a Powerful and Ethical Public Voice

In times, where the use of abuses and foul language is considered to be the 'new cool', it is important to emphasize the role of civil language and ethics to invite greater discussion and participation. Some of the most important insights we have gathered through our discussions with scholars, teachers and parents over the years involves using sensitive language and focusing on 'similarities' between people rather than magnifying differences. Though it is important to understand our differences and realize that they are real, very often people acknowledge that there are more similarities than differences in them!

Although social media provides a lot of opportunities, it also presents threats and dangers. Critical use of social media involves both harnessing the potential and avoiding the dangers. In the following section, we discuss some of the threats related to the Internet and social media use among children and suggest ways in which parents and educators can make young people aware of these limitations.

HOW TO BE SAFE IN AN INTERCONNECTED WORLD?

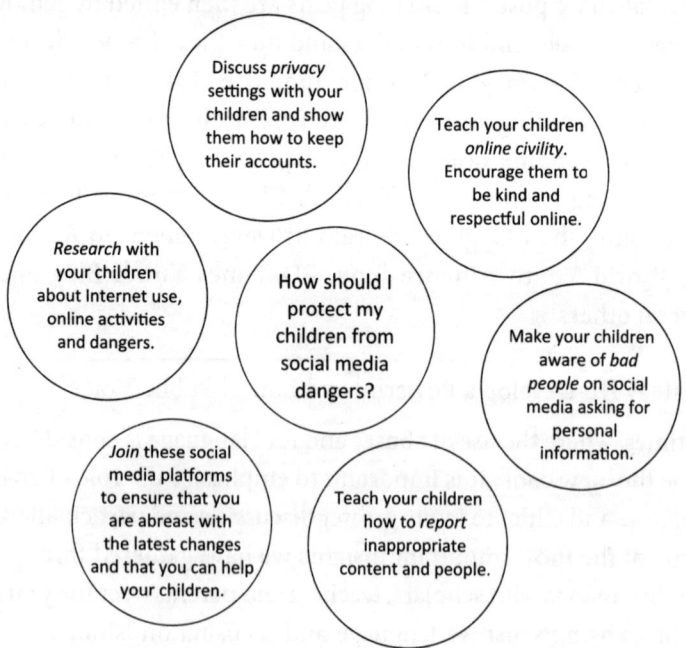

Discuss *privacy* settings with your children and show them how to keep their accounts.

Teach your children *online civility*. Encourage them to be kind and respectful online.

Research with your children about Internet use, online activities and dangers.

How should I protect my children from social media dangers?

Make your children aware of *bad people* on social media asking for personal information.

Join these social media platforms to ensure that you are abreast with the latest changes and that you can help your children.

Teach your children how to *report* inappropriate content and people.

Before we plunge into devising ways to protect our children from the perils of the Internet use and social media, let us understand these possible threats in detail. According to UNICEF's Child Online Protection in India report, one in every three children with access to the Internet and social media experiences some form of cyberbullying, cyberthreats or breach of privacy. In some other cases, these children are the online offenders—harassing, bullying and threatening others. The technological affordances of social media, especially anonymity and the resulting deniability/distance, may embolden many young people and adults into offensive and criminal online activities.

There are five main forms of online abuse and exploitation that we need to be aware of.

1. *Cyberbullying:* This includes emotional harassment, social exclusion, defamation, social exposure or revelation of private details and intimidation.

2. *Online sexual abuse:* Circulation of sexually explicit messages about someone, leaking their personal photos or videos, extending rape threats and revenge porn.

3. *Cyber extremism:* Ideological indoctrination, threats of violence and encouraging children to become violent.

4. *Online commercial fraud:* Identity theft, hacking, phishing and financial fraud. Here, phishing refers to the fraudulent practice of sending e-mails purporting to be from reputable companies in order to persuade individuals to reveal personal

information. Similarly, catfishing is the practice of creating a fake online persona that offenders use to communicate with others on social media.

5. *Grooming:* Preparing a child and and an online environment for sexual abuse and exploitation.

Children and young people will encounter these threats more than once in their digital engagements. Instead of panicking and banning Internet use for children, it is always better to educate them about ways to protect against their dangers on social media. We know that crossing the road involves the risk of getting hit by a vehicle, but we don't stop our children from crossing the road ever, do we? We handhold them in the beginning, teach them how to do it safely and make them aware of the rules. It is the same with the Internet.

There is a three-pronged approach that we propose to enable our children to counter social media threats.

1. Internet discipline
2. Transparency
3. Digital literacy

Let us look at each of them in detail.

Internet Discipline

It is impossible to keep our children away from the Internet, especially the social media. When children have access to technologies, the Internet and social media, they sometimes refuse to accept the authority and experience of their elders—teachers and parents—in learning how to navigate through these gadgets and networks. They also think that they know more than us! The first step towards protecting children from social media threats is to create a routine of discipline. It is advised that parents are aware of their children's net-based and social media activities and practices. Many educators suggest using shared devices for education and entertainment until the child turns 16 years or above. Instead of granting your child a personal laptop, parents can consider installing a desktop in a shared space—the study room, which can be assessed by all members in the family. The second strategy can involve mutually deciding on the number of hours children are supposed to spend on their gadgets and social media for both entertainment and education. When this limit is mutually agreed upon, parents must make extra efforts to respect these limits and not assume unhindered access to gadgets because of their authority and position in the family. Rules that apply to children should be applicable for the parents as well; for example, no gadgets during meals. Third, mutually decide the correct course of action for making amends every time someone flouts the generally agreed upon rules related to the use of social media and the Internet.

Transparency

We have interacted with some parents who find it very difficult to accept that their teenage children are watching porn online. Here, it is critical to note that the Internet use of young children must be strictly monitored to protect them from inappropriate content and dangerous people, but we should also be ready to accept that, as children mature, they will use these devices for intimate and personal purposes. To ensure transparency with children, discuss safe ways of using the Internet with children. Introduce children to the idea of incognito windows but also discuss with them the consequences of uploading private photos online as any online repository and storage can be easily hacked. Help your children navigate away from violent porn and discuss how watching aggression and violence can create unrealistic expectations in their minds and eventually harm their relationships. At the same time, also allow them to explore things on their own.

Many Indian parents snoop into their teenage children's phones and call them out for a text they sent, a message they wrote or photos they shared on their Instagram. If parents use an authoritative approach to control their children's social media use, children will find more discreet ways of hiding their online life from their parents.

Remember, they are not obliged to share their passwords with you, and there are umpteen ways of holding multiple secret accounts on the Internet. So if we want to protect our children from possible dangers and threats, we must try to develop a rapport with them, understand their world that has changed from when we were their age and make them trust us so that they are ready to share their online spaces and activities with us.

Digital Literacy

Digital literacy includes the active process of equipping children and young people with information about the threats involved in using digital media, especially the Internet and social media. We also familiarize children with the resources to avoid, challenge and report them. Before allowing children to access social media, parents must hold a detailed discussion with them related to all possible perils of using social media uncritically. Parents can use different examples to discuss the consequences of cyberbullying, online sexual abuse, identity fraud and other cyber threats. A strategy to create awareness among children about cyberbullying and other issues is to hold 'co-viewing' sessions where parents and children can watch documentaries, shows and stories about the dangers of using the Internet and social media uncritically. The intention is not to scare them, but to prepare them well. For children above the age of 12 years, the first season of '13 Reasons Why' can be a good starting point to initiate discussions around bullying, sexual abuse, exploitation, threats and privacy topics.

STRATEGIES FOR FIGHTING CYBERBULLYING AND ONLINE ABUSE

- Teach them to never post or say anything on the Internet that they would not want the whole world—including you—to read.

- Talk to them about reaching out to an adult at the first sign of a threat. Kids refuse to confide in their parents because they're scared that if the parents find out about cyberbullying, they will take away children's Internet or cell phone.
- Teach your children that something posted online can become public and cause unimaginable pain and suffering. If they see or witness something problematic online, they should report it. Not reporting amounts to being complicit.
- Encourage kids to speak out against bullying when they see it. Popular sites such as Facebook and YouTube provide tools to report inappropriate content, and the 'comments' features associated with individual pages can provide opportunities for witnesses to speak out.
- Do not fight back. A lot of times the bullies are looking to get a rise out of the kids they are targeting and fighting back just gives them what they want.
- Document and save the evidence. Tell your children to make sure they have a record of what happened if somebody is mean to them online. If it is something that was sent directly to them, make sure they save it. If it's something that can be deleted (a tweet, a status update, etc.), encourage them to take a screenshot.[4]
- Talk to somebody. Your children should have access to people and other helpful resources if they want to report bullying. Equip your children with helpline numbers and encourage them to approach their counsellors in schools.
- Remind them that it is not their fault if they are being cyberbullied. Nothing they do makes it okay for people to be mean to them, and nothing about them justifies people being mean to them.

---

[4] http://www.take-a-screenshot.org/

It is extremely crucial to remind your children of the consequences of bullying others to ensure that they do not become the perpetrators. Monitor your children's online activities to make sure they are not involved in any online fraud, identity theft and other criminal activity.

As we examine online activities and engagement of children, we must also pay attention to the narratives of online games children play. Sometimes, these online games are extremely violent and aggressive. Such games encourage using online abuses and normalizes discursive violence. Also, some games are not age appropriate. It is, therefore, necessary that families create a healthy media diet and follow it.

DESIGNING THE FAMILY MEDIA DIET

As parents, we take great care in planning healthy meals for our children. A healthy media diet is just as important. The first quality we should reflect upon and embrace is 'digital discipline'. Digital discipline largely refers to our use of digital technologies and platforms. It constitutes the time we spend browsing the Internet, scrolling through our social media profiles and pages, watching movies, listening to songs and podcasts, and so on. Parents and children can create a timetable delineating their digital use so that each member of the house is allowed to access gadgets, technologies or social media for a limited amount of time. It is also crucial to ponder on the concept of a 'sacred space' which is devoid of any technological intrusion. This sacred space, such as the dinner table or the library or the bedroom, should ideally allow family members to engage with each other in the complete absence of any technological mediation. For instance, parents may choose to leave their phones at home when they take their children to parks, hotels or movie theatres.

A rich family media diet must include a good mix of co-viewing and personal viewing practices. Co-viewing strategies are very effective in helping children interpret media messages and online activities. Even if it is not possible to commit to a co-viewing practice, parents can ask their children about what they watch and read.

It is equally important to plan non-media activities for the family. Many times, children turn to their gadgets because of boredom, loneliness and lack of other interesting activities.

QUESTIONS PARENTS CAN ASK TO MONITOR THEIR CHILDREN'S MEDIA CHOICES AND INTERPRETIVE SKILLS

- Tell me what happened in the show.
- What did the characters do?
- Do you agree with what the characters did? Why or why not?
- What did the characters talk about?
- How did you feel watching the show? Why?
- What was your favourite part? Why?
- What part did you not like? Why?
- What questions do you have? (e.g., meaning of words and actions of characters)

Creating a family media diet includes accessing three things: how much time are we spending on media technologies; why are we using media technologies, that is, the purpose? And how can we include diversity in the media we are consuming as a family—genre, content, issue, origin and other topics?

The time criterion decides the amount of time a family spends on the media. According to many studies, young people should not spend more than two hours per day on digital media. Creating shared ground rules for how long in a day can children and parents use digital media is a democratic process because it will involve discussions and shared decision-making. Another strategy is to block out a large part of the day to a 'no digital media' use. For instance, in many families, no one can use their phones and laptops before heading out for work and after coming home. Some people also install applications that set the daily usage limit of various social media platforms to no more than 2 hours per day. Second, in today's technological world, most of us rely on our gadgets for work and education. Dividing the time spent on gadgets for work and leisure purposes can help us save the time we waste scrolling through others' profiles, watching memes for hours at a stretch or substituting playing video games over visiting playgrounds or parks. Finally, analysing and actively selecting meaningful content to further the growth and well-being of our children through media consumption is a very important step. The media provide avenues to discuss social issues, unburden us through humour or inspire us to work more efficiently the next day. Media experiences can be both critical and grounding in nature. We can choose to watch, read and listen to media designed to challenge our thought processes and to force us out of our complacency towards ourselves and our communities. Of course, we use the media to relax, laugh, escape in fantasy worlds and bond with other family members over shared programmes. There are thankfully many films, shows, podcasts and over-the-top content that combine fun with sensitivity. Some media narratives reinforce the status quo in societies and reify discrimination. If we are not vigilant, we may fall prey to media narratives that are produced only to generate revenue without any regard for the mental well-being of viewers. Many shows on Indian television, for instance, perpetuate patriarchal and misogynistic behaviour, and this can be detrimental to the growth and progress of our communities. Our minds are like our bodies; we must be very careful of what we put in them.

CHAPTER 8

Art with a Purpose

SOCIALLY ENGAGED ART PRACTICE

Do you remember attending a performance that stayed with you for days or weeks or shook you up? Do you remember listening to poetry or seeing a painting that made you sensitive to issues you had never thought about because they didn't directly impact you? Do you remember a film that opened a completely new angle to look at marginalized groups such as Dalit women, the elderly or refugees? Art can have a powerful impact, and many activists believe in reaching out to people through art.

We have strong memories of a performance we had witnessed by Ahmedabad-based 'Budhan Theatre' members. The Budhan Theatre is run by youth from the Chhara community. The Chhara are one of the de-notified tribes who were nomads and were labelled as habitual thieves. Youth from the community have suffered much stigma and discrimination because of this label. Their play 'Budhan Bolta Hai' opened our eyes to the atrocities and oppression such marginalized groups have to face. Based on real-life experience, the play raised serious questions about justice and challenged our silence.

Art historian Claire Bishop[1] defined the term 'socially engaged art' as art practices and activities that aim to engage with the society and people. Socially engaged art pays close attention to identifying problems and issues related to the society and living in communities. It is a grounded approach and relies on the observation, immersion and bringing about a change within immediate communities and relationships. Socially engaged art enables people to 'imagine' a better future for their communities, build intergroup relationships and improve social systems.

[1] C. Bishop, 'The Social Turn: Collaboration and Its Discontents', in *Right about Now: Art and Theory Since the 1990s*, eds. Margriet Schavemaker and Mischa Rakier (Amsterdam: Valiz, 2007), 58–68.

The focus is on harnessing people's imagination and encouraging them to think of new and novel ways of resolving problems through artistic activities. Socially engaged art practice involves creating a learning environment conducive to innovation, problem-solving and thinking out of the box.

There are three ways to recognize socially engaged art. They are as follows.

1. *Imaginative:* Participants are encouraged to expand the horizon of possibilities related to how to live, interact and engage with issues and others in our societies. It encourages to think outside the box, or sometimes even to smash the box!

2. *Change-oriented:* Socially engaged art practice aims at helping others imagine 'change' through art and activism. The focus is on enabling viewers to conceive change as possible and as achievable. Also, this form of art tries to bring about a change in both the society and the process of creating art.

3. *Participatory:* Socially engaged art practice is generally collaborative in nature. It either invites participation on the part of viewers or on the part of artists–participants collaborating to co-create an inclusive social message.

Do you recognize these three qualities in the following example? It is drawn from one of our media literacy and art projects with children.

THEATRE FOR HINDU–MUSLIM UNITY[2]

In a school, theatre workshops were held with school students belonging to Hindu and Muslim communities in India. In the

---

[2] K. Bhatia and M. Pathak-Shelat, 'Using Applied Theatre Practices in Classrooms to Challenge Religious Discrimination among Students', *Journal of Adolescent and Adult Literacy* 62, no. 6 (2019): 605–613.

community where this school is situated, the Hindu–Muslim intergroup relations are tense and sensitive. Media educators encouraged students to address the issue of Hindu–Muslim relations using theatre as a site of imagining ways to reduce the felt differences and tensions between these two religious communities.

Students were encouraged to write a script for the play, enact the script and stage it for their community. Students wrote a script trying to address three important issues: (a) everyday practices of discrimination among one group towards the other, (b) ways to reduce instances of discrimination and (c) invite the audience to participate in thinking of ways to improve intergroup relations between Hindus and Muslims.

In this project, students used their imagination to think of possible ways of being, and of developing cordial Hindu–Muslim relations. This enabled them to question their biases and prejudices, even if temporarily, and imagine a situation where peaceful coexistence between Hindus and Muslims is possible. Second, they used theatre to bring this imagination into existence through a script and performance.

Hindu and Muslim students collaborated on this project as teammates; they worked together and resolved their differences to create meaningful art. This helped them see their teammates in a different way—as talented writers, actors, fun partners and thinkers rather than just as a person of a certain religion. Students also invited their community members to witness this enactment of a different possibility, encouraged them to practise change in their communities and to work towards improving Hindu–Muslim relations.

We do not claim that participating in and witnessing one art production changes things forever. Socially engaged art practices, however, have certainly become a real factor in humanizing people, connecting them through stories and bridging differences through collaborative meaning making. They reveal a vision of what a better world can look like. Socially engaged art practices are a form of storytelling; narrating stories about a future where people can coexist, differences can be overlooked for the collective good and people are treated as humans and not as one-dimensional religious, caste, class and gender monoliths.

According to Anna Hickey-Moody,[3] a professor at RMIT, art can be a channel, a means through which we can change our body's capacity to feel, think and be involved. She introduced a term 'affective pedagogy' which implies that we can use art to change our bodies' capacity to act in particular ways. This pedagogy has three core teaching principles. First, learning happens when young people experience and practise ideas or concepts in actual physical spaces, such as homes and schools. Any teaching–learning strategy should be sensitive to the needs, aspirations and realities of young people. Children and young people must feel, experience and invest in the learning process in order to initiate a change in their societies and in themselves. Second, learning through creating art; it involves harnessing the potential of 'action', 'doing', 'making' and 'experiencing' change. In other words, when young people are equipped with the skills to practise art and make visible an alternative future of inclusive and peaceful societies, they become 'change agents'. They produce a change in the art they create and adopt an 'active' role in the change-making process. Many researchers and educators suggest that when children (or adults) are involved in the process of initiating change, they are

[3] Anna Hickey-Moody, 'Arts Practice as Method, Urban Spaces and Intra-Active Faiths', *International Journal of Inclusive Education* 21, no. 11 (2017): 1083–1096; Anna Hickey-Moody, 'Affect as Method: Feelings, Aesthetics and Affective Pedagogy', in *Deleuze and Research Methodologies*, eds. Rebecca Coleman and Jessica Ringrose (Edinburgh: Edinburgh University Press, 2013), 79–95; Anna Hickey-Moody and Mia Harrison, 'Socially Engaged Art and Affective Pedagogy: A Study in Inter-Faith Understanding', in *Tate Papers*, no. 29 (Spring 2018). Available at https://www.tate.org.uk/research/publications/tate-papers/29/socially-engaged-art-and-affective-pedagogy (accessed on 12 September 2020).

more inclined to continue their movement towards the betterment of our societies. 'Initiating change' through art is therefore a critical process of thinking about alternative and peaceful futures. Once young people have the skills required to identify and resolve problems through art, they will continue to use artistic forms of expression to imagine and articulate new future possibilities. Finally, artistic sites such as theatre, dance, posters, videos and others are excellent spaces for collaborative work.

LISTENING AND RESPONDING TO DIFFERENCES

Can art be used to respond to differences? Can art be used to encourage young people from different sociocultural backgrounds to work together? How can we design and implement cross-cultural/religious/caste/class projects to bring young people to work together?

Many scholars suggest that activities designed to bring different people together so that they can work on tangible goals that are more than leisure and entertainment can be the starting point. Such activities enable children to step away from their discriminatory framework of reference and to see the other on the basis of their personal experience of working together. Using art as a site of 'collaborative work' is effective because it treads the narrow path between serious work and leisure. When children are required to work on art projects for reward and recognition, they are motivated to collaborate with others on the basis of merit, skills, and interest. Also, intergroup collaboration is easier to begin when there is a purpose—some 'work' involved and not just play. For instance, a child belonging to a wealthy community may feel uncomfortable initiating contact with their classmate belonging to the lower income community for fun and entertainment. The child may feel awkward inviting their classmate to their house just for 'fun' or 'play'. This is because these children have lived in a highly segregated society and inter-class friendships are not something that people strive to experience. In this scenario, inviting children to participate in an art project may give them a sense of purpose and alleviate their anxiety. It is also easy to convince other adults when it is an art project.

Here, it is important to acknowledge that the process of unlearning, teaching our young people differently and raising them in a more inclusive society is not a straight line from point A to B. There will be many hurdles, and we will have to accept that many of these may seem unsurmountable. We cannot expect ourselves or our children to wake up one day and practise non-discrimination towards others. We will have to deal with our hesitation, reluctance, and doubts.

In the art project modules that we design for children, parents and educators, we acknowledge that it will be a slow process. People are not predisposed to have a sense of love, affection or care for the out-group. It is a critical task to cultivate imagination because we will have to train ourselves and our children to develop, feel and express care and respect for others. In the following sections, we identify different forms of socially engaged art practices and suggest ways in which parents and educators can use these to create inclusive spaces and counter caste/class/religion/gender-based discrimination among young people. These activities can be adapted for classrooms, communities, clubs or camps.

WORKING TOGETHER AMID DIFFERENCES

Socially engaged art practices developed in this book focus on three learning goals:

1. Creation of shared artworks
2. Developing a shared understanding about religious, gender, caste and class differences through collaborative art making

3. Enabling children and parents from different social groups
   to initiate meaningful conversations in ways that encourage
   empathy, mutual respect and understanding

Through these art projects, we will be creating counter-spaces
that challenge the otherwise segregated nature of our cities and
communities. This process will compel us—adults as well as young
people—to imagine what it might mean to inhabit an interfaith/
caste/class/gender community.

As educators and parents, we acknowledge that a sense
of belonging binds members of communities and this sense of
belonging is infused with historical, symbolic, cultural and geographical realities. Some traumatic historical events, such as
the partition, have left their marks on many generations. For
instance, for members of a Gujarati Hindu community living
in Godhra, their perceptions about the 'Muslim' community
are influenced by the memory of communal conflicts (history),
the segregated nature of all-Hindu and all-Muslim neighbourhoods (geography), the presence and access to temples and
mosques (symbolic) and the celebration of shared festivals such
as Uttarayan (cultural). Similarly, the perceptions of young men
and boys about girls and women in our societies may be influenced
by the role of their mothers, grandmothers and other women in
their own families (history), the way in which women and girls
are treated, represented or appear in public spaces such as metros,
parks and streets (geography), the way in which women and girls
are portrayed in popular culture such as movies, theatre, books
and other narratives (symbolic), and the prevalence of patriarchal
thought process in different facets of our lives and societies (cultural).

As is evident, most of these experiences, embedded in
different layers of history, culture, symbol, geography and others,
are specific to a given individual or community.

Misperceptions emerge and biases against each other take
a strong hold when people cannot access and understand these

nuances in other peoples' lives, cultures and societies. Collaborative artwork is expressive; it allows people from different backgrounds to express these layers to one another, to identify points of similarity and to blend these together to create art pieces. Collaborative artwork can become a means of reinvigorating intergroup exchanges and a strategy for imagining inclusive futures.

In the following sections, we develop some socially engaged arts practice project ideas that parents and educators can modify to suit their local requirements.

Artwork at School

Most schools in urban cities of India have designated 'arts and crafts' classes in the school curriculum. Also, most schools dedicate some number of classes to discuss and cover topics on community development, social work and character development. Annual days and festival celebrations also provide opportunities for collaborative art projects—plays, open mic or spoken word, designing murals or displays. Educators can think of ways in which they can use these opportunities to design 'socially engaged art practices' workshops and projects for children and teachers. Workshops provide an introduction on the aim and intention of the projects crafted for children.

WORKSHOP I. INTRODUCTION TO SOCIALLY ENGAGED ARTS PRACTICE

Phase I: Begin the workshop with a 'brainstorming session' on understanding the role of art in bringing about a change in our communities. Some starting questions can include but are not limited to:

1.   What does art mean to you? Give us some examples.
2.   What is the role and importance of art in our lives?

3. What happens when we create and make art?
4. Do you have to be good at art to enjoy it?
5. What kinds of art activities do you enjoy participating in?
6. What kinds of art activities can we do in groups and collectively?

Discussions around these questions will help educators understand their students' artistic interests.

Phase II: Help children identify and think through some of the very critical problems facing our communities. For instance, discuss with them the issue of gender equality, respect for different classes, castes and religions. Now, help them think how they can use art to address these issues. An example is given as follows:

Issue: Giving equal opportunities to girls and boys
(Questions to think about: Why is this issue important? How will addressing this issue change our societies?)

Art activity: Writing and staging a play (theatre)
(Questions to think about: Why use theatre? How will this contribute towards bringing about a change?)

Groups: Three groups (scriptwriters, actors, managers) consisting of both girls and boys, ideally from different backgrounds (why is it important to work in groups consisting of both girls and boys, and from different backgrounds? How will the group members resolve differences in opinions? How will they manage conflicts?)

Drawing from our experiences of working as media educators, we wish to provide an example of the responses we got to the questions included in our module for Workshop I during our interactions with students from Grade 8 from a school in Ahmedabad.

RESPONSE TO WORKSHOP QUESTIONS OF GRADE 8 STUDENTS

Phase I

1. What does art mean to you? Give us some examples.
   We enjoy art. It relaxes us. When we are too tired of studying, we do art, such as dance, paint and all. Also, when we feel stuck, like if there is a math question we cannot solve, we do some art activities and then try to work again. Sometimes, art gives us new ideas, especially about how to solve a problem, like a math problem.

2. What is the role and importance of art in our lives?
   Art is everywhere around us, isn't it? Our arts and crafts teacher told us that we can find art—something to paint, everywhere…no matter where we are, we can do something with it and turn it into art. To be honest, if art weren't around, we would be so bored and dull. Art is so colourful… not just colours in the literal sense, but how artistic it is. We do not know how to express this correctly, but you know what we are trying to say, right?

3. What happens when we create and make art?
   When we make art, we feel very happy and we want to show it to everyone. It feels good if someone looks at what you have made and maybe says something about it. It shows the person was paying attention. Some people make art for themselves, but most people do it because they

want to show it to the world, to others. What is the use of art if you cannot exhibit it to others? See, if movies were made just for the people making it, they would be so useless. So it means that movies, music and many other activities can be called art.

4. Do you have to be good at art to enjoy it?
   We think everyone should make art. We can show it to our close friends and family, and not to everyone, but the fun is too much. It is fun to sit with friends and colour, draw or do something else together in class. And it also means we get to escape from studies for a little bit.

5. What kinds of art activities do you enjoy participating in?
   Cooking, drawing, painting, drama like we do on annual days in our school, rangoli making, we also have poster making competitions, some girls in the group stitch and make clothes and many others embroider. All these activities are artistic in nature.

6. What kinds of art activities can we do in groups and collectively?
   We can do plays, drama and dance, singing, painting, poster making, embroidering or making flowers from coloured stocking and candle making.

Phase II

Issue: Giving equal opportunities to girls and boys

1. Why is this issue important?
   Half of our population is girls, so if we do not give them good opportunities and they cannot contribute to society, we will be lagging behind. Both boys and girls are important, but boys have more freedom and choices, and girls are often

ignored. Many families favour their boy children over their girl children, and that is not right. Sometimes boys also feel a lot of pressure, and they can't choose activities or careers of their choice.

2. How will addressing this issue change our societies?
    If boys and girls are given equal opportunities, we can have a merit-based society, and everyone will be able to contribute towards its development. If everyone in the family, for instance, is educated they all can contribute equally to build their families. Our literacy rate will rise if girls are educated, our income will increase if girls have equal opportunity to work and all. Everything will become better.

Art activity: Writing and staging a play (theatre)

3. Why use theatre?
    All of us have seen a play or have participated in one. Every year, for the annual day, our school puts up a play performance for parents. It is fun to do. When we are doing a play, time just flies, and those who watch it remember the story. Miss Kalpana once said that when we do a play, we will remember its teaching and the story after many years. So we are more comfortable doing a play.

4. What will happen if children write and enact a play on this theme?
    First, we will have to find out more information on this. We do know a few things, but to write a play we need more information, details and all. Then we will think of a story keeping in mind what we have in this class. We cannot write a play about space for instance. We will have to discuss what we learn about this topic and we will try to look for answers and solutions for this issue.

5. How will this contribute towards bringing about a change?
   So, first of all, when we think about it, we will learn new things on how to solve this issue. Whatever we learn, we will put it in a script and enact it, but as we do that we will also be able to express what we feel about these problems. We will have to ask girls in our group more about what their problems are. We have never had that discussion. Some people think that girls and boys talking is gross, but when we work in groups, we will learn so much more about each other. That will be nice.

Groups: Three groups (scriptwriters, actors, managers) consisting of both girls and boys

6. Why is it important to work in groups consisting of both girls and boys?
   Boys do not have to face the same problems that girls have, but we are so shy and so afraid to talk to each other that we never ask. In these groups, we will have time to learn about such problems and develop ideas to solve problems. If we do not have boys and girls both we will never be able to present both sides correctly. What if the girls believe that boys are useless, and they do not help but we are not like that? Girls will get to know us and know that maybe we are different.

7. How will the group members resolve differences in opinions? How will they manage conflicts?
   We have planned on creating a shared group rule. Every person will be given a chance to share their opinion through role-taking. If someone has problems, they can talk about their problems very calmly. They should not hurt others. We will include ideas only when 80 per cent of the group agrees. Moreover, we have decided to listen to others. We will try and not talk too much and all day.

As is evident through the response sheet, these brainstorming sessions will help educators and children understand which art activity is appealing to their students and work around them to discuss, stage, present and debate ideas, creating inclusive societies and spaces. When children from different groups work together to produce art, often, the produced piece of art represents ideas related to inclusivity and civic ethics, such as justice and equality. These can be used as sites to initiate meaningful dialogue among the larger groups of parents and community members. Also, many scholars emphasize that in collaborative interfaith/caste/class/gender teams, while engaging with the issue at hand, children learn critical negotiation skills because each team member would have a different way of looking at the issue. They learn how to articulate their opinions and ideas, how to debate without being rude or aggressive and how to find an acceptable solution in multicultural groups. For this, they must tailor their ideas in ways that appeal to the sentiments of different people in their groups. Children in such collaborative projects also learn to listen to different opinions respectfully and to accommodate these differences in the best possible way. Children can also learn how to be attentive and sensitive to the experiences of others in their groups.

We describe this as a process in developing critical empathy among children. Critical empathy involves taking into consideration the other person's perspective. It involves understanding how others feel when they are discriminated against, when they are not given equal opportunities, and when they are denied the right to live with respect and dignity. In this, students listen to others and learn to relate with a wide range of experiences.

Let us look at another theatre activity that we designed to help children in interfaith groups and classes develop sensitivity towards different religions and cultures in our society.[4]

---

[4] This activity was developed for students in interfaith classrooms and has been previously published in the *Journal of Adult and Adolescent Literacy*. Bhatia and Pathak-Shelat, 'Using Applied Theatre Practices in Classrooms', 2019.

LET US TAKE ACTION!

1. Ask students to create a list of the religious differences they observe in their classrooms, especially related to issues such as clothing and food habits of the religious other.

2. Ask students to critically think how these differences in relation to their classmates who belong to a different religion influence their interpersonal interactions with others. Then, encourage students to work in interfaith groups of five or six and discuss their observations.

3. On the basis of these discussions in interfaith groups, ask each group to develop two staged scenes of discrimination that they face in their classrooms, such as religious slurs, not being allowed to participate in games and not sharing food with others.

4. Ask students to witness this performance and suggest ways in which the scenes can be changed. In other words, ask the student participants to interrupt the scene representing discrimination to change the situation by suggesting solutions to challenge discrimination and improve interfaith relations.[5]

Collaborative art projects for social change are participatory not only in terms of those involved in their production and creation but also in terms of those who observe and watch these pieces later, that is, the audience. In one such project, organized by Professor Anna Hickey-Moody in Australia, children from different religious backgrounds produced large papier-mâché objects—creating large symbols of their faith. The children were then asked to paste these different symbols of religious beliefs and values that they had created together on globe model decorated with LED lights.

---

[5] For more information read *Theatre of the Oppressed*. Augusto Boal, *Theatre of the Oppressed* (New York, NY: Theatre Communication Group, 1993).

These globes, created together, represented a world of shared beliefs and values where every religion had its rightful place to thrive. Throughout the process, children from different backgrounds started bonding over the art-making project, helping one another to cut and paint symbols, asking many important questions, learning more about each other's faith and understanding the traditions of other faiths. Professor Hickey-Moody explains:

> Many of the symbols of faith seemed quite stereotypical, representing 'Eid' and celebration of 'Diwali'. But others complicated relationships between religion and belief. For example, a female, vegan, Muslim participant drew a basket of eggs as a 'stop' sign with a cross through it, showing that part of her personal belief system involved not eating animal products. Other children struggled to connect what they saw as abstract principles of their religion to their life, but often happily settled on shared beliefs such as 'being kind to people', and 'being clean'.

In yet another project that we undertook with students in schools of Ahmedabad, we introduced them to the idea of drawing 'body maps'. Body maps are an abstract representation of one's bodies created through painting, sketching, drawing and other art-based techniques to visually illustrate aspects of people's lives—their feelings, emotions, beliefs, values and so on. Body mapping is a way of telling stories about ourselves to each other through art. In this project, we encouraged students from different backgrounds to create a shared 'body map' highlighting the things that were most important to them in their lives. Their body maps revealed a beautiful tapestry. For instance, children from a very affluent background drew symbols of materialistic things on the body map, such as video game remote, watches, iPhone and speakers, while children from a middle to lower economic background inscribed words representing community life and shared resources. They wrote words such as 'langar' and drew the activities that they play with friends like hide and seek and the streets they loiter. Although these words represent differences in their backgrounds, they also had several common experiences, such as reading books, travelling by rickshaw or cab to school, eating samosa at the school canteen and the importance of friendship and play. This was followed by a discussion among the participants explaining the importance of things they drew in their lives. It helped them realize that the clothes they wear, the products they use and the way their bodies appear in classrooms are influenced by where and how they live. Such dialogues can provide children access to realities that are different from their own and thus make them aware of the limitations of others. A deeper examination of these also led them to see systemic injustice and to realize why the poor mostly remain poor and the rich become richer.

Such experiences of working together can be a point of locus to invite parents to participate in the process of change. The artworks created through these projects can be presented to the parents either as an exhibition or as a performance. For instance, drama can be staged during school festivals, and parents watching the show can be encouraged to submit their responses and feedback to the school drama committee. Similarly, posters, murals and paintings made through such socially engaged collaborative processes can be exhibited and parents can be invited to join a live discussion about the exhibition with student artists.

What is interesting to note is that such fun and insightful art projects can extend beyond classrooms and be adapted for homes and community gatherings. In the following section, we highlight some strategies to initiate a socially engaged arts project at home with children.

Artwork at Home

Our home is one of the many places where we practise segregation intentionally or unintentionally. Is it possible to reorient our children and encourage them to engage with topics of shared interests while also addressing uncomfortable questions around religion, caste, class and gender in our homes? How can we redesign our home spaces to involve greater participation from children with different cultural backgrounds?

We had in-depth interactions with children and parents in the urban areas of Delhi, Ahmedabad, Bangalore and Mumbai, and we asked them to identify the most common problem related to different communities hanging out together. Given further is a list that we compiled on the basis of their responses.

When asked what were their apprehensions in encouraging students to engage in intergroup activities, the parents said they were

1. Uncomfortable with differences in food habits (very commonly observed in vegetarian families)
2. Afraid of the assumed low levels of cleanliness and hygiene (often referred to when parents were discussing caste and class differences)
3. Afraid of girls and boys developing physical intimacy (in mixed gender groups)
4. Fearful that their children might get influenced by the other's culture, religion or traditions
5. Scared that their children may have unreasonable demands related to goods and products if they hang out with high-class children
6. Unsure if the other children's neighbourhoods were safe (this was especially true for Hindu middle class or upper-class

parents when they had to discuss the possibility of allowing children to hang out with their classmates who were Muslims and/or from a low economic background)

7. Worried about what their relatives and community members will say if they allow their children to be friends with those from outside their community

8. Averse to this idea, because they simply did not like the other's community (this can imply that they were prejudiced and refused to engage with their biases)

We certainly understand that all parents would be concerned about their children's safety, but we realized that many of these fears were not based on their actual experience. This led us to make the following two observations:

1. There is little to no meaningful interaction between people from different castes, classes, genders and religious communities.

2. There is a strong push from within our communities to compel us to limit our social contact largely to in group members.

In such situations, parents must take a lead in initiating a process of change in their homes and altering the segregated nature of their houses. As this is a difficult project and consists of creating safe spaces where such dialogues can be voiced, we suggest that parents resort to art-based practices to open their homes, courtyards and neighbourhoods to those from outside their local communities. Art-based practices and workshops provide a constructed sense of 'purpose' to these intergroup gatherings and associations. These activities alleviate the stress and conflict arising from asking parents and children to engage with someone different just for 'fun'. Also, this constructed sense of purpose is meaningful because other parents can use this to convince their families and communities that intergroup gatherings are required and essential. Children will learn to paint, draw, dance, cook and so much more.

We draw from our work as media educators to suggest three art projects designed to invite children from different backgrounds to frequent your homes thus enriching you with novel under-standings of different cultures, rituals and lifestyles.

Turn Your Home into a Digital Arts Lab

Even in urban areas of India, not every child has access to the Internet for learning and educational purposes. Inviting your children's classmates to your home and encouraging them to use online digital arts tools under parental guidance and supervision can be a very effective way to start conversations about gender, caste, class and religion-based issues with the help of technology. Let us take a look at some of the digital art-making activities.

Activity 1: Writing a story about harmony and peace

Online tool: Story Bird[6]

Story Bird is a free online storytelling website that can be safely used by children of all age groups.

Guidelines:

- Invite your children's classmates to hang out at your home for making digital art.
- Randomly assign them to different groups of 4 to 5 children to ensure that children from different backgrounds get to hang out and learn together.

---

[6] https://storybird.com/

- Show them the introductory video on how to use this website to create their own stories.
- Ask them to write their own stories using the resources available on topics such as 'peace', 'religious harmony', 'equality' and 'freedom'. You can also find fun ways to address these topics.
- Ask students from different religions to explain how their religious texts and teachings discuss these topics.
- Ask children to answer the question: How do our religions define togetherness, peace, harmony and equality? How can we include these ideas in a story? What images can we use to illustrate these ideas?

Screenshot of a project created with our students using Story Bird.

Activity 2: Narrating stories about everyday routines and lives

Online tool: Story Jumper[7] is a free to use website for children of all age groups.

Guidelines:

- Form 4–5 member groups consisting of children from different castes and class backgrounds.

---

7 www.storyjumper.com

- Ask them to define caste and class.
- Now, ask them to share their experiences of belonging to a particular caste and class in their societies. For instance, what does it mean to belong to the Brahmin caste or the Dalit community? What does it mean to live in a high-rise building? What does it mean to walk or bike to school to save transportation cost? What does it mean to sit in a classroom with others who have the latest gadgets or products? All these questions will emerge as students start narrating their routines and everyday lives.
- Record these stories and use the website to juxtapose them over each other. For instance, the experiences of an upper-caste boy can be juxtaposed with the narration of a lower-caste girl to understand how caste and class influence the everyday realities and experiences of people.
- Substitute these narrations with symbolic pictures to create a multimedia story.

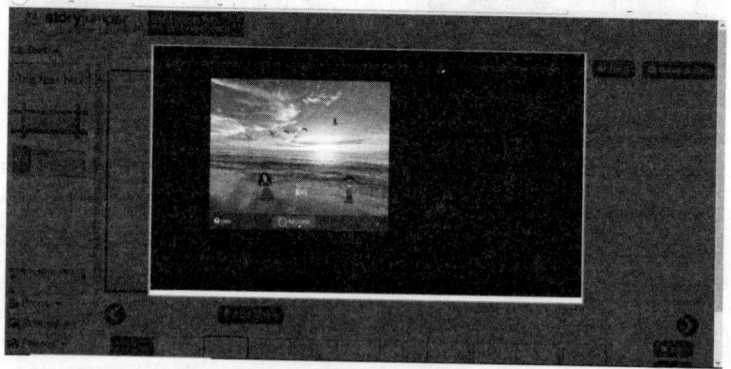

Screenshot of a project created with students using Story Jumper.

Take Your Little Artist Groups on the Streets

The differences between groups and the segregation of communities is a phenomenon that manifests itself in physical forms, that is, in what we can see and observe in our spaces if we pay critical attention to our surroundings. We are raised to trust and internalize things that we see around us every day. For instance, when children are raised in a higher class neighbourhood, the infrastructure and amenities they witness and observe all around them reinforces their conviction that upper class community existence is ideal and pristine. In the absence of exposure to the world outside these gated communities, children would feel repelled and averse to the idea of visiting and spending time in non-gated, less affluent neighbourhoods. Some may even label these neighbourhoods as dirty and unsafe. As is evident, class status is reinforced by what we observe around ourselves and what we see every day. The visual aspect of our everyday lives informs our ideas, values and beliefs about ourselves and others. What we see every day is normalized and becomes acceptable, while that which is hidden from our routines of observing and seeing becomes either inaccessible or wrong.

The question then is: will introducing our children to the observable aspects of alternate lifestyles and rituals help them realize that their way of being in the world is not the only way?

In our educational projects with schoolteachers and students, we used 'participatory photography' to help young people think of alternative ways in which they could challenge the segregated nature of their neighbourhoods, streets and community spaces. Before we elaborate more about this project, let us understand a little about participatory photography.

PARTICIPATORY PHOTOGRAPHY

Participatory photography is a technique of giving people access to cameras so that they can record their life experiences and their voices. It allows them to

a. Narrate their own stories
b. Use the right to author new stories defying previously held opinions and beliefs on the basis of new things they observe and document
c. Imagine a different possibility by adopting a new way of looking at things and recording those observations for others to learn from them.

Participatory photography has the potential to change our 'field of visibility', that is, what we see, observe and normalize. It has the potential to add new layers to our visual experiences. It has the potential to break a conflict cycle by allowing different groups to think and illustrate what an alternate and inclusive future will look like.

We draw from our project to suggest ways in which parents can use participatory photography to introduce their children to new ways of seeing and new norms of being.

PHOTOWALKS: GENDER AND STREETS

Background: In 2015, a collective of women students organized a movement called 'Pinjra Tod' to reclaim public spaces and streets and make them safe for women. Their aim was to challenge the dominant assumption that public spaces are not safe for women and so women must be protected. This group of women decided to throng the streets, create more noise by occupying streets in large numbers and normalize the presence of women in public spaces to emphasize that these sites cannot be controlled by men.

Activity: Invite your children and their classmates to participate in a photowalk through the streets of their neighbourhoods and communities under parental supervision. The project teams thus formed must consist of both girls and boys. Give them the following guidelines:

- Identify a few streets and corners where you have heard that it is not safe for girls and women to visit.
- Identify a few places in the city where there are very few women and many men.
- Visit these sites and places, and photograph people walking on the streets, standing in the corners, visiting shops or offices.
- Back at home, discuss these photographs. Try addressing these questions: are there differences in the way men and women appear on the streets? What were men doing on the streets—actions, facial expressions, gestures, comfort level, dress and clothes, and so on? What were women seen doing on the streets—how were women behaving on the streets? If you are a girl member, how did you feel when you visited places occupied by more men and very few women? Do the things that you see on the streets make you feel safe? How can you change that?
- In another photowalk, invite more girls to the group and visit spaces where there were fewer women. Crowd these spaces dominated by men with more girls—mothers, sisters, friends and others, and observe how this changes the dynamics of the space. Try documenting the presence of these women on the streets and observe if there is any

change in their behaviour compared to women documented during the previous photowalk. Also, try examining how the appearance of more women in these spaces influence the behaviour of men? Is there a change in the way they walk, talk or the activities they do? Is there a change in their outward expressions, gestures and body language?

- Conduct a brainstorming session to understand how increasing the presence of girls and women (visual) in public spaces can help them feel safe and more comfortable about being in public. Think of possible ways in which this can influence the way men interact with women on the streets.

- Organize a photo exhibition at the school where photos from these photowalks are displayed and encourage other classmates to identify and debate the differences in the photos from the two photowalks.

PHOTOWALKS: RELIGION AND OUR CITIES

Rationale: Our popular culture and everyday life are full of instances that highlight religious conflicts, discrimination and biases. We have discussed how our residential areas in cities are segregated on the basis of religion—Hindus and Muslims live in very different neighbourhoods, Christians have their residential areas in the cities and Jains may refuse to allow any other community, especially if they eat meat, to exist in their vicinity. In such situations, what we observe everyday are the segregations and so practicing differences is normalized. It is, therefore, crucial to identify and appreciate the already existing inclusive and interreligious spaces in our cities.

Activity: Children should be taken out for a one-day trip to explore all the sites in our cities that bear testimony to interfaith harmony and coexistence.

Guidelines:

- Ask children to use the Internet, study the history and culture of their cities and identify sites that symbolize unity among the different groups living there.
- Visit these sites with cameras and record symbols on these sites that exemplify unity and peaceful coexistence. For instance, in the city of Ahmedabad, the Sabarmati Ashram often organizes an all-religion prayer ceremony on its grounds to mark solidarity between different religious communities in India. Similarly, the Dargah of Pir Haji Ali is worshipped by members of various religious communities; the Haji Ali Dargah is a revered place for both Hindus and Muslims. Reading about these places, the multicultural history of our country and visiting these to develop a perspective on what coexisting looks like can be extremely rewarding.
- Capture photographs of these places in ways that reinforce interfaith belongingness.
- Make these photos reflecting the possibility of interfaith existence a part of our everyday visual diet, that is, pin them on the walls of the rooms, or make them a desktop wallpaper and so on.

Although these two project ideas use religion and gender as a topic around which photowalk activities are designed, the same principles of participatory photography can be used to change the normalized and observable instances of caste- and class-based discrimination in our societies. Let us take a look at the following suggestions for some other possible projects:

- Children can be encouraged to create photostories documenting how excess or lack of material wealth and social status influences their lifestyles and everyday routines. Bring in photostories of students from different backgrounds and weave them together in a huge exhibition. Allow children to ask questions about how these differences based on class are created, sustained and reinforced. This will give them an opportunity to devise plans to forge personal relationships that can bridge class barriers.

- To discuss caste-based discussion, ask children to work in inter-caste groups and, through discussion, identify five everyday instances where children from lower castes face discrimination, while children of higher castes enjoy their privileges. Some examples through which lower caste children are reminded of their caste status can be media reports and news on issues related to untouchability and violence against lower castes in several parts of the country. Similarly, instances of practising privilege can include, but is not limited to, instances of families mistreating house helps, cleaners and sweepers, and public sanitation workers. Encourage children to document these instances through photographs and to record stories around these photos. This can be a multimedia exercise where photographs are accompanied by a narrative provided by children on how they observe and experience caste in their everyday lives.

As is evident, we can use an art-based approach to redesign our homes and classrooms, and convert them into safe spaces for our children to imagine, practise and experience an alternative future of care, belongingness and compassion for all. Socially engaged arts practices serve a twofold function. First, they are participatory and collaborative in nature, making it feasible for children from multiple backgrounds to coexist and work together towards shared interests and purposes in interesting ways. Second, the artefact created through such a collaborative process is a testimony to what a shared future of mutual understanding and peaceful coexistence can look like. In imaging such a future, we conceive and experience new actions, behaviours, language and feelings that are integral to its creation.

CHAPTER 9

As We Say Goodbye

As we end this exciting and challenging journey, we would like to share the thoughts, feelings and experiences that have gone into writing this book. It has been a difficult book to write, precisely because these are times when what is going on in the world makes us question the wisdom in being kind, fair and critical. We question the wisdom of raising our kids to embrace vulnerability and share power when everyone else is clamouring for it. We have constantly made efforts to ensure that this book does not become preachy and utopian, but rather speaks to the real challenges of parenting in these difficult times.

When we were just beginning to write this book, our friend Sujata confided in us about a dilemma she was facing as a parent. Her son, Saral, had been coming home crying and bruised from the playground for the last few days. He narrated how a playmate harassed him and beat him every day on the playground. 'Why didn't you do anything', Sujata screamed out with distress. 'Because Ma, you only told me that I should not indulge in *maramari*, be nice to my playmates and tell an adult if there is a problem. I told his mom, but she didn't say anything to her son.'

Sujata did not know what to say. Her own advice had put her son at risk. While discussing this, Manisha shared a lesson she learnt from her family. Her brother was the youngest in the class and a tiny child. He often got bullied by older boys. That is when Manisha's father had to change his views on how to teach children to resist. These were his new instructions: one, never be the first to raise your hand; second, never beat up anyone who is weaker and smaller than you and, third, if you get beaten and the person is not open to reasoning, you have to defend yourself. You can choose to be non-violent only if you are strong; putting up with abuse because you are weak and do not have the strength or courage to fight back is not non-violence.

So our advice is not that you teach your children to turn the other cheek when they get slapped on one. We believe that we should stand up for our rights. At the same time, we believe that if we are strong and capable, we can do a lot to make the society a better place for everybody. With that purpose, we would like to reiterate a few important points that we have been stressing upon throughout the book.

1. Getting out of the box
2. Understanding systemic discrimination
3. Developing competences in using non-violent ways of resolving differences and practising them
4. Participating in creating a larger social fabric that values harmony and social justice

GETTING OUT OF THE BOX

We should respect our core values and cultural wisdom. A lot of our received wisdom, however, might have been relevant in the time when it originated, but is completely irrelevant for today's times and context. Do not hesitate to question. Also, allow your children to question anything and everything. Of course, long discussions, arguments, at times, temper tantrums are difficult undertaking, especially when compared to the say alternative of saying 'shut up' or 'because I say so' or 'because this is how it has always been'. It is worth the effort though. Be open to accepting changes that make sense or bring dignity and rights to people who have long been discriminated against. Feel free to hold on to your opinions, but check where they are coming from. Read, travel, watch thought-provoking films and shows, and get first-hand experiences of people and places. Experience different virtual communities and get a glimpse of the lives of people who are very different from you.

There are valuable insights to gain from those who think starkly different from us, so please do not shut yourself and your children within your comfort zone. In this respect, we have seen many 'intolerant tolerants' who claim to be liberals but cannot tolerate any argument challenging their way of thinking. So maintaining open channels of communication is a great way of getting out of the box.

UNDERSTANDING SYSTEMIC DISCRIMINATION

For understanding systemic discrimination, we must take a long-term view and look back at our history. Discrimination, to put it very simply, is injustice, violence, exclusion, denial of benefits and rights, and an unfair burden that individuals and groups have to face because we label them based on their class, caste, race, gender, religion, ethnicity, age, disability and so on. Systemic discrimination severely impacts their well-being and survival. When such practices continue unquestioningly and unchallenged for years—from generation to generation—because powerful groups and individuals benefit from this arrangement, they get normalized. Gradually, we all feel that this is how things have always been and will be, and there is discrimination because of some fault of these individuals and groups. This is systemic discrimination—discrimination that becomes such an integral part of our system that it seems normal and acceptable.

This is not to say that people who face discrimination are never wrong or that they never engage in discriminatory behaviour towards other groups. Sadly, many times we see that people who have been oppressed become oppressors when they gain power and engage in similar discriminatory behaviour instead of working towards creating an inclusive society. As an individual, even if you belong to a privileged group, it is likely that someone from the underprivileged group has hurt you or discriminated against you or your children. We cannot negate anyone's experience and feeling of hurt, and we should stand up against anyone who is bullying us.

Here is the catch though. When we are so overpowered by this one experience, we forget how so many individuals and groups have faced such treatment for generations, and only because they carry a certain label. This understanding will help put things within a broader perspective.

It is helpful to be kind to people who have faced discrimination and abuse. We can certainly begin with empathy and kindness, but that is not enough. Difficult and uncomfortable questions about systemic discrimination must be asked and acted upon. For example, do we think of the deaths of Dalits in custody in India when we protest the death of George Floyd in the USA on social media? We are wise to check our own privileges and entitlements before we judge others.

VIOLENCE IS NOT THE SOLUTION

Our children's safety and well-being are paramount. They should be strong and competent to take care of themselves. Violence, however, never solves any problems. No one is safe in a violent society. It just sets into motion a vicious cycle of revenge and hatred. Also, violence is not always physical. Aren't we all a witness to trolling, demonizing and vilifying that happens on social media just because someone holds a different opinion or has made life choices that we do not approve of?

You might ask, do I not have a right to hold on to my ideology? My opinions? Yes, of course, though we hope that your thinking helps in creating a more just and inclusive society. You also have the right to win people over to your thinking. Whatever it is that you passionately support, and you have strong reasons to support it, there are non-violent ways of doing it. Persuasive communication can drive people to identify with and endorse your arguments—you can blog, use social media, friends and family conversations, be a media talking head, write opinion pieces or make videos. And encourage your children to do the same.

Children would benefit much by joining grassroots organizations that develop skills in public speaking, working with diverse groups, problem-solving, developing coherent arguments and interacting with the media. Also, if media and writing are not your children's forte, art is another option.

Young adults can also impact public thinking by voting: voting for the right political candidates, voting with money and supporting brands, organizations, companies and local business that genuinely care about social welfare and are fair to their workers and our environment; voting with the remote, that is, not supporting films or television shows that are demeaning to certain groups or spread negative stereotypes while also encouraging positive media.

STEPPING INTO THE FUTURE

Ultimately, we understand that raising children who are open yet critical, strong yet compassionate, who believe in freedom and yet respect other people's rights is never going to be an easy task. It is a rewarding and exciting process though, and it is more so when we make forgiveness an integral part of this process. We forgive ourselves, and we forgive others. We get up again when we stumble and help others to stand tall with us.

We hope that this book will be a conversation starter and help us to initiate difficult dialogues and discussions in our families, communities and schools. We hope that our paths cross again and that we can continue this engagement. As we say our goodbyes, we leave you with one of our favourite fables.

A monk was standing on a seashore. He would pick up the fish that got thrown on the shore with the high tide and put them back gently in the water. A passer-by saw this and watched for a while, perplexed. When he could not control his curiosity, he asked the monk, 'what are you doing?' 'I am saving these fish from dying by putting them back in the water,' the monk replied. The man scoffed at the response and said, 'There are thousands of them that die on the shore every day. Would a handful you save make any difference?' To this, the monk smiled serenely, picked up one fish from the shore, gently placed it in the water and said, 'Well, it made a difference for THIS fish!'

ABOUT THE AUTHORS

Manisha Pathak-Shelat is Professor and Chair, Centre for Development Management and Communication, MICA, Ahmedabad. She believes in a scholarship that is socially engaged, accessible and global in scope. She considers her work in academia a way to make meaningful contribution towards a better world through teaching and writing. It is also her space to meet interesting people, have enriching conversations and engage in stimulating collaborations that often transform into deep friendships.

She has a PhD in mass communication from the University of Wisconsin-Madison, USA, and a PhD in education from the Maharaja Sayajirao University of Baroda, India. She has taught and worked as a media consultant, communication trainer and researcher in India, Thailand and USA. The common thread that connects her work is exploration of how ordinary citizens engage with media and use communication to experience agency, explore identities and participate in social change. Manisha has published her work widely, presented it to audiences globally and received prestigious awards and fellowships. Her other books include a co-edited volume titled *The Handbook of Media Education Research, Communication for Gender Sensitization: The Value Discussion Approach*, a set of 12 energy and environment stories for tribal children of Gujarat and a co-authored book with Kiran Vinod Bhatia titled *Challenging Discriminatory Practices of Religious Socialization among Adolescents: Critical Media Literacy and Pedagogies in Practice*.

She loves working with and writing for young people. She chooses to take the scenic route to life, savouring small joys and adventures. Travelling, gardening, reading, listening to music and dancing are her de-stressors and, of course, long family vacations.

Kiran Vinod Bhatia is a doctoral candidate in the School of Journalism and Mass Communication, University of Wisconsin-Madison, USA. A critical digital ethnographer by training, her scholarship largely explores the links between social networking sites, digital affordances and the global digital cultures of young people in India. Her work has been published in the *Journal of Children and Media, Journal of Youth Studies, Journal of Communication Inquiry, Asian Journal of Communication, Journal of Adolescent & Adult Literacy* and *Contemporary South Asia*, among others. She has worked with school students, village/town communities and high school teachers in several parts of Gujarat, India, co-creating/conducting media education classes with them. She has co-authored a book based on this project, *Challenging Discriminatory Practices of Religious Socialization among Adolescents: Critical Media Literacy and Pedagogies in Practice* (2019).

Her research draws force from the desire to dismantle systems of oppression and violence in our societies. She believes that critical education and thinking have the potential to change the ways in which we engage with others and our lived realities.

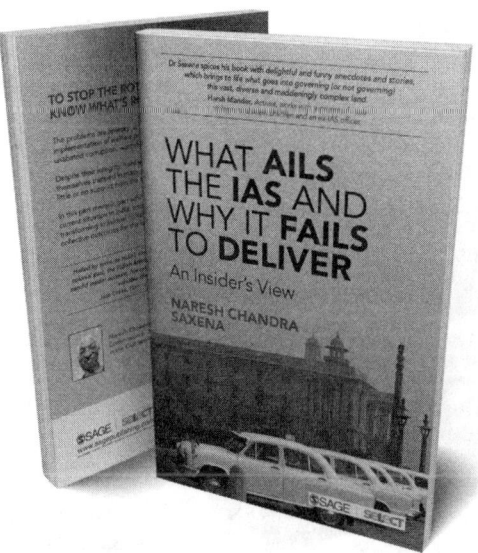

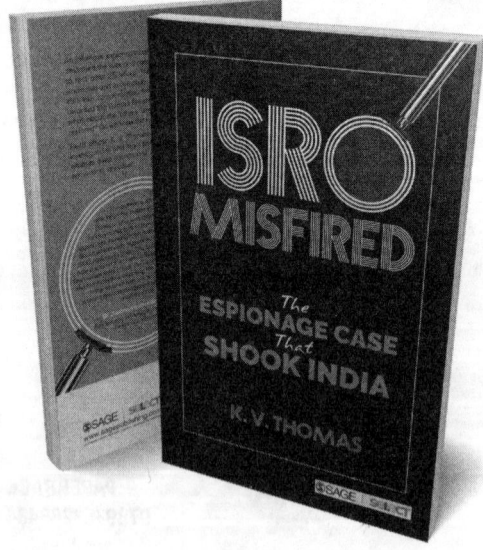